YORK NOT

General Editors: Profess
of Stirling) & Professor
University of Beirut)

D. H. Lawrence

SELECTED SHORT STORIES

Notes by Neil McEwan

MA, B LITT (OXFORD) PH D (STIRLING)
Lecturer in English, Okayama University, Japan

 **LONGMAN
YORK PRESS**

YORK PRESS
Immeuble Esseily, Place Riad Solh, Beirut.

LONGMAN GROUP UK LIMITED
Longman House, Burnt Mill,
Harlow, Essex CM20 2JE, England

First published in 1991

ISBN 0-582-06565-8

Produced by Longman Group (FE) Ltd
Typeset by Gem Graphics, Trenance, Mawgan Porth, Cornwall
Printed in Hong Kong

Contents

Part 1

Introduction

The author's life

David Herbert Richards Lawrence was born at Eastwood, a colliery town in the Nottinghamshire countryside, in 1885. His father was a coal-miner, uneducated but a good story-teller, a dancer and nature-lover, and a man of energy and warmth. His mother, a former teacher, had married for love, but soon came to resent her husband's coarseness. The five children grew up in a divided, often violent home. David Herbert (the fourth child) was impressed by his father's stories of the mines, but was closer to his mother, especially in adolescence after she had nursed him through a serious illness. *Sons and Lovers* (1913), Lawrence's third novel, portrays, in the hero's love for his mother and her inhibiting possessiveness, the author's own experience, which is also reflected in many of his short stories.

He owed much to his mother's ambition for her children. Regular attendance at chapel and Sunday school gave him a thorough knowledge of the Bible, whose style and imagery were to influence all his writings. The chapel's Protestant, Nonconformist tradition helped to form Lawrence's blend of moral seriousness and unconventionality, and – as he recognised – a tendency to preach. At the age of twelve, urged on by his mother, he won a scholarship to Nottingham High School. He became a pupil-teacher in 1902, and, after two years (1906–8) at Nottingham University College, a schoolmaster in Croydon.

He read widely during these years and discussed what he read with Jessie Chambers, a friend from a farm near his home; she encouraged him and helped with his earliest poems and often clumsy attempts at short stories. He lost his faith in Christianity, and began to develop his own religion – venerating 'all gods' and the 'true nature' of Man – which was to inspire his whole life and work. He began to publish short stories in 1910. His first novel, *The White Peacock*, came out in 1911, full of faults, yet impressive, and, Lawrence said, 'all about love'.

In 1912 he met Frieda Weekley, the wife of a Nottingham professor. Frieda came from a German family (the von Richthofens). She left her husband and children for Lawrence and they married in

1914. The marriage was stormy but secure. After the appearance of
Sons and Lovers, Lawrence found recognition and friends in literary
London. Ford Madox Ford (1873–1939) – formerly Ford Madox
Hueffer – who published some of Lawrence's earliest stories in the
English Review, had already hailed him as 'a big genius'. By 1914, the
year of his first volume of short stories, *The Prussian Officer*,
Lawrence had given up teaching because of illness, and become a
professional writer.

The outbreak of war, which affected him deeply, brought practical
problems: he returned from Germany (where he and Frieda had been
living) and moved through various parts of England, unfit for military
service, but suspected by the police, partly because of his German
wife. He hoped to go to America to found a new type of community –
a project called 'Rananim' which interested him all his life; but in
1917 he was refused a passport.

He planned a novel which would be more original, in method and
approach, than his previous work. Provisionally called 'The Sisters',
this became *The Rainbow* (published in 1915) and *Women in Love*
(written in 1916). The first edition of *The Rainbow*, considered
obscene by most reviewers, was destroyed by a court order. The first
English edition of *Women in Love* was brought out, despite attempts
to suppress it, in 1921. Throughout these years he worked at short
stories, publishing a second collection, *England, My England*, in
1922.

After the war, the Lawrences travelled abroad, moving from
Florence and Sicily to Ceylon, Australia and New Mexico; he died of
tuberculosis in France in 1930.

His later novels and stories continued to study the relations
between the sexes (with a boldness that often offended). The best
of the later novels are *The Plumed Serpent* (1926) and *Lady
Chatterley's Lover*, which was not published unexpurgated in
England until 1960. *Kangaroo* (1923) is concerned with social and
political problems. He continued to develop the art of the short story
in the 1920s, publishing another collection, *The Woman Who Rode
Away*, in 1928. His stories have always been considered a major part
of his achievement. His output was prolific: he published over fifty
books – poems, short stories and longer tales, essays, travel books,
and polemic. He was a lively and provocative reviewer of the books
of his contemporaries. He was also a painter with a flair for colour,
an able teacher, a good talker, and a keen observer of nature
and of human life. He was intrigued and inspired by exotic and
ancient cultures (especially Aztec and Etruscan), though his
imagination was dominated by the English Midland scenes of his
early life.

Lawrence could be infuriating in his dogmatism and combative-ness, but his energy and charm, humour and courage were always attractive. He could be naive (as he was in dismissing most philosophy and science) in advancing his own creed of 'the blood', 'the dark gods' and 'the man alive'. He was at his best a visionary; at his worst he could be tedious, and the discipline of the short-story form suited his art in curbing his tendency to 'preach' (his own term). He believed in his talents and was dedicated to the full use of them, and through this dedication he made himself a part of our modern literary culture.

General background

The coming of railways and coal-mines transformed rural Nottinghamshire in the course of the nineteenth century. Lawrence's early stories show how close the life of the countryside was to that of the mining communities, but they also show changes. In early Victorian times, squire and vicar had been revered as figures of absolute authority; but when the Colonel rides by a group of miners in 'Strike-Pay', they ignore him, although they admire his horse; the vicar in 'Daughters of the Vicar' is treated with little or no respect when he arrives in a mining parish. The Industrial Revolution brought, on the one hand, new forms of hardship, danger and ugliness to the lives of the English poor. Miners were often killed or maimed at work, and a lifetime in the pit could destroy a man's health. Lawrence thought the enforcement of ugliness on the lives of ordinary people one of the worst offences of the Victorian mine-owners. Industrialisation, on the other hand, also extended the possibilities of life. The old miner in 'The Christening' is physically disabled, but one of his daughters, 'the lady of the family', is 'a college-trained schoolmistress'. The independence and knowl-edge of life which girls were beginning to achieve in the early decades of the century would have been incomprehensible to earlier generations, who lived as farmers and farm-workers, close to the land.

Lawrence hated many of the results of English industrial and urban growth. He loathed vulgarity in all social classes, and the materialism and conventionality which he thought enfeebled the 'tough old England that made us'. He was also very critical of modern intellectuals. As a young man he absorbed the radical ideas of earlier generations: the theory of evolution in *The Origin of Species* (1859) by Charles Darwin (1809–82); the psychology of Sigmund Freud (1856–1939); and the philosophy of Friedrich Nietzsche (1844–1900) – anti-Christian, 'Dionysian', supporting man's animal instincts against

'Apollonian'* rationalism. Lawrence was influenced by such reading but he also fought against it. He despised all ideologies and systems which led people away from morality as he understood it – truth to one's own manhood or womanhood. It took him time to work out his own philosophy, but from the start of his career he was dissatisfied not only with modern social conditions, but also with much of modern thought.

Socialism was one creed popular among intellectuals, and Lawrence was infatuated with it for a time. In 1915 he wrote to the philosopher Bertrand Russell (1872–1970) that the framework of society must be 'smashed' and everything nationalised. But he quickly became impatient with socialism. The First World War disillusioned him. 'In 1915 the old world ended', he wrote later in *Kangaroo*. He felt that mankind had succumbed to a shameful hatred; belief in progress was discredited. His contempt for middle-class 'respectability' and his sense of the corruption which comes from possessions are plain in many of his stories, but his ideas were more concerned with how to live than with how to organise society.

Like other thinkers of the time, Lawrence saw the First World War as a crisis for the whole of Western civilisation. He feared that Christian societies, grown so deeply materialistic, had come to have 'a death wish'. Even their idealisms were inextricably linked with materialism – as he urged in the story 'Things'. The war was a sign of a terrible imbalance in modern culture. His thought developed in terms of opposites: mind and body; conscious and subconscious experience; intellect and emotion; sensuality and spirituality (and paganism in contrast to Christianity); law and order (especially in institutions such as the Army and Navy) and instinctive, natural life; middle class and lower class; male and female. These opposing principles can be seen throughout his fiction. 'Daughters of the Vicar', for example, contrasts the middle-class vicarage and the Durants' cottage, the intellectual Massy and the sensual, unthinking Alfred, the disciplined life of the Navy and the freer life of the pit. Lawrence was not 'on the side of' the body against the mind, or in favour of the unconscious, instinctive, sexual forces in man against reason; nobody thought or reasoned with more resolution and enjoyment. But he believed that the English middle classes had erred on the side of a constricting 'respectability', and that imbalance is dangerous in all life's partnerships.

In some ways, Lawrence was fortunate in living when he did. He benefited from the advance of free schooling after the Education Act

---

*The two terms were first used by Nietzsche in his *Birth of Tragedy* (1872) to represent two opposing sides of human nature: Dionysian is the primitive, passionate, instinctive side of man, while Apollonian stands for the civilised, rationalist aspect of man.

of 1870; the educational standards of his time were high. The gradual 'breaking down of social barriers', to which many of his books refer, allowed him to move relatively easily through English society. Stories such as 'The Rocking-Horse Winner' portray upper-class life. Although many of his novels and stories treat relations between the sexes – often presented as a conflict, as in 'Monkey Nuts' and 'Tickets, Please' – with a frankness which would have been completely unacceptable in the nineteenth century, he managed to publish most of his work in spite of the censors, and to find a readership. Travel, except during the war, was relatively easy. He lived in circles where freedom of thought was taken for granted.

'His problems were central to a main current of growth and difficulty in our society and our culture', Raymond Williams wrote in *The English Novel from Dickens to Lawrence* (Chatto and Windus, London, 1970, Chapter 8). The emancipation of women, the effects of industrialisation, class relations in a democratic society, personal freedom in a modern state – issues which are faced by the characters of his fiction – are still problematic today.

Literary background

Lawrence's critical writings show a broad knowledge of English, French, German, Russian and American literature, and frequent impatience with almost all earlier writers. Because he learned from so many examples, and because he was so determined to obey his own instincts as a writer and not produce 'imitations' of other people's books, it is difficult to point to precise influences. He seems to have feared falling under the intellectual influence of the great Russian novelists Leo Tolstoy (1828–1910) and Fyodor Dostoevsky (1821–81). He attacked what he called the 'complaint' of excessive preoccupation with formal beauty in the fiction of the German Thomas Mann (1875–1955) and the Frenchman Gustave Flaubert (1821–80). Yet he is clearly indebted to these European writers and to English fiction from Jane Austen (1775–1817) to Henry James (1843–1916), both of whom he disparaged at times. Some critics maintain that his strong moral sense derives from the English tradition in fiction; others that his awareness of social relations was acquired from English novels. It was necessary, though, for Lawrence to disown traditions in order to clarify what he wanted to write.

George Eliot (1819–80) and Thomas Hardy (1840–1928) are the English novelists with whom he has most in common. Both came from the provinces; both made themselves familiar with European culture; both brought keen intellectual interests to the writing of fiction. They shared a love of nature and a sympathy with uneducated people; they could see historical processes in English life, and show private acts against a social and universal background. Lawrence resembles them in these respects; but in reading him there is no sense of imitation.

He both learned and distanced himself from other writers of short stories. In England, H. G. Wells (1866–1946) and John Galsworthy (1867–1933), good social observers and intellectually well-informed, were artists in this genre. Lawrence considered that they wrote 'good stories' in too traditional a way, well-plotted and thoroughly organised, implying a world where all is known and in its proper place. Katherine Mansfield (1888–1923), his near contemporary, was, under the influence of Anton Chekhov (1860–1904), the Russian dramatist and master of the short story, more experimental. She avoided sensational events and relied very little on plot; instead she explored in sensitive, poetic prose the human meaning of small events. Lawrence, who knew Katherine Mansfield (and her husband John Middleton Murry (1889–1957)), shared (as did most writers of fiction in their generation) her wish to escape from the nineteenth-century 'tyranny of plot', and he too wanted to explore the possibilities of images and symbols; but he wrote a looser, and more insistent, more open and vigorous type of fiction, suited to conveying his ideas.

A note on the text

The stories discussed in detail in these Notes are those in *D. H. Lawrence: Selected Tales*, introduced by Ian Serraillier, New Windmill Series, Heinemann Educational Books, London, 1963. They are summarised in Part 2, and discussed in the section 'Nature, purpose and achievement' (where dates of publication are supplied) in Part 3, in order of first publication. Some other well-known stories are discussed in Part 4.

Summaries
of SELECTED SHORT STORIES

'Odour of Chrysanthemums'

Section I

Elizabeth Bates is waiting for her husband Walter, a coal-miner, to come home from work. It is late afternoon in winter, and miners are walking back from the pit. Elizabeth calls her five-year-old son John in from the garden. The boy scatters petals of pink chrysanthemums on the path; she puts a spray of flowers to her face and then wears them in the band of her apron.

Railway lines run close to the house. Elizabeth's father stops his steam-engine by the gate and calls for a cup of tea. She is not pleased that he is to marry again so soon after her mother's death. He says that Walter has been drinking too much lately in public houses.

It is four-thirty. Watching John carving wood, Elizabeth sees in him her husband's 'indifference to all but himself'. She tells herself indignantly that Walter must have gone straight from work to drink in a public house. She snaps at her daughter Annie, home from school. When she and the children sit down for tea, the room is dark except for the red glow of the coal-fire, which John likes to watch. Annie exclaims with delight, seeing the chrysanthemums when her mother lights the lamp, and smells them; but her mother rebukes her, grumbling about Walter's drinking. Tonight he can lie on the floor in his pit-dirt, she says. The children play, 'united in fear'. Walter is still not home when they go to bed. Elizabeth sits alone, angry and beginning to be afraid.

Section II

At eight o'clock, fear drives her out of the house. Unwilling to enter a public house to look for her husband, she goes to see neighbours. Mrs Rigley, another collier's wife, asks her in. Treating Elizabeth with respect because, as we notice from her speech, she is an educated woman, Mr Rigley says he will look for Walter in a nearby pub.

Elizabeth waits at home, until her mother-in-law arrives with news: Walter has had an accident. She begs Elizabeth, who is five or six months pregnant, to be calm. She recalls how jolly Walter was as a boy, and says one must 'make allowances' for men. A collier comes to say that Walter has been killed, smothered when trapped by a fall of coal. The women find comfort in tears. Moving the furniture ready for laying out the body, Elizabeth notices a 'deathly' smell from chrysanthemums in vases in the room.

The pit-manager, Matthews, arrives at ten o'clock, with two colliers bearing the dead man on a stretcher. One of the men breaks a vase of flowers. Unable to look at Walter's body, Elizabeth fusses over mopping up. Annie calls down, and her mother says that they have 'brought' her father – as in the past when he was drunk. She goes up to the children to tell them that Walter is asleep. The men hurry away. Wife and mother strip and wash the body. Handsome and pale, the dead man fills the women with dread and with other conflicting emotions. His mother is sure he died in peace, and recalls how he used to laugh as a boy. Elizabeth feels that she has never loved her husband; the child in her womb is 'like ice'. She and Walter never knew each other, even when making love. She thinks how wretched the loveless marriage must have made him. The women dress and cover the body.

Elizabeth submits to life, but, in the last words of the story, 'from death, her ultimate master, she winced with fear and shame'.

NOTES AND GLOSSARY:

whimsey:	a hoist
Brinsley:	Lawrence's father worked at this colliery, near Nottingham
turned up:	brought to the surface
chrysanthemums:	flowers of a late-blooming (autumn and winter) garden plant
mash:	make tea
bout:	heavy drinking
half a sovereign:	ten shillings; a sovereign was a gold coin worth a pound, last generally issued in 1917
twenty-three shillings:	that is, for a week's housekeeping money. In the British currency in use until 1971, there were twenty shillings to a pound, and twelve pence to a shilling. Other coins included the farthing (until 1960; four to a penny), the sixpence, the florin (two shillings), and the half-crown (two shillings and sixpence). In colloquial speech, a sixpence was a 'tanner' and a shilling was a 'bob'. In Lawrence's lifetime, sterling had approximately twenty times its present purchasing power. Sums

	of money in 'Strike-Pay' give an idea of the cost of living for the poor; those in 'The Rocking-Horse Winner' reflect the spending of the rich
settler:	problem
metals:	rails
fender:	low metal frame around a fireplace
hob:	metal shelf by the fire
'cos:	because
ripping:	cutting the roof of a seam of coal
wafflin':	(*dialect*) waving
crozzled:	(*dialect*) burnt
canna:	cannot
'Asn't e:	Hasn't he. Unlike Elizabeth, Mrs Rigley speaks in dialect, 'dropping aitches', and using local (and old) forms such as 'childer' for children
squab:	padded seat
'Asna 'e come whoam yit:	Hasn't he come home yet? Mr Rigley's dialect is broader than his wife's
'appen:	(*dialect*) perhaps
stint:	day's work
Loose-all:	the signal to stop work
Bowers:	a miner
thinkin . . . bantle:	(*dialect*) thinking that he was just behind and that he would come up in the next batch of miners
Dick's:	the 'Yew Tree', another public house
butty:	(*dialect*) mate or buddy, but among coal-miners, a senior miner trusted to deal with officials and employers
chiffonier:	low cupboard with table-top

'Strike-Pay'

Ben Townsend, the Union agent, is distributing strike-pay to miners in the schoolroom of the Primitive Methodist Chapel. The men are in good spirits, enjoying the excitement of the strike and the prospect of a holiday. A group sets off to watch a football match in Nottingham: John Wharmby, who can play any musical instrument; fat, smiling Chris Smitheringale; Sam Coutts, who has received an extra two shillings because his wife had twins the previous Monday; and Ephraim Wharmby. They walk across country, stopping in villages to buy rounds of beer. It is a fine spring day. When the Colonel rides by on his splendid horse, they ignore him, boasting to each other of how miners will soon come out on strike all over the world. They stop in a field where pit-ponies are at large; Ephraim and Sam ride the ponies,

showing off their agility. Further on, Ephraim says that he has
dropped his half-sovereign, the ten-shilling coin which is strike-pay
for the week. A search in the meadow yields nothing. With shame,
Ephraim accepts the others' offer to share, taking two shillings from
each. They stop at a public house in Bulwell. Here they bet on the
skittles matches, Sam winning enough to pay for lunch. Notts, the
team the men support, win the football match.

Ephraim leaves his friends, who mean to go on celebrating at the
'Punch Bowl'. On the way home, he sees an accident: a workman has
been stifled in mud. He senses that death, and the strike, are greater
issues than the battle he faces now. He and his wife Maud, married
for two months, live with his mother-in-law, a fierce widow, 'very
erect, very dangerous'. She attacks him with 'polite' English, and he
takes refuge in broad Derbyshire. He proffers five shillings and
sixpence from the six shillings his friends gave him. The mother-in-
law now launches into abuse of him: four shillings and sixpence spent
in a day on drink and women! At last he is provoked into shouting
back at her, and she leaves the house. Maud makes him a cup of tea,
and warms up his dinner. He is *her* man, not her mother's.

NOTES AND GLOSSARY:

Primitive Methodist: this sect broke away from the Methodist Church
in 1810

crier:	a crier would go round the streets of a mining town, calling out news
pouches:	folds in the clothes
Sorry:	(*dialect*) pal, mate
A bob a kid:	an extra shilling is paid for each child. For currency, see notes and glossary to 'Odour of Chrysanthemums'
thysen:	(*dialect*) yourself
rag:	play the fool
best suit on:	'with his trousers on', according to the usual version of this nursery rhyme, read out solemnly here as though the first lines of a hymn to be sung in the chapel
addled:	(*dialect*) earned
be-out:	(*dialect*) without
gleamy:	(*dialect*) sunny
Sithee:	(*dialect*) look!
ostler:	stableman looking after the pit-ponies
simbitar:	(*dialect*) in the same way. The sight of the Colonel intensifies the men's dialect
cassivoy:	(*dialect*) pond

skewbawd:	a skewbald horse is white with any other colour except black
foraged:	searched
beside your jacket:	in you
usboard:	our board and lodging
on the nines:	smartly dressed
Ripping:	acting like tearaways
trollops:	woman of no self-respect

'The Christening'

Hilda Rowbotham is proud of her status as a college-trained school-mistress, although heart disease makes her a ridiculous figure in the street: small, thin and striding slowly as though she were more than her actual age – not yet thirty. When she buys cakes at Mr Berry-man's, the baker embarrasses her by asking sarcastically about her younger sister, Emma. She feels ashamed as she walks back the length of the main street, although pride enables her to look unconcerned.

Her home is a large cottage built by her father, an old coal-miner, from his life savings. Emma is cutting bread and butter in the kitchen. There is a 'downcast, humble' expression on her 'heavy, brutal' face. She is an unmarried mother, and has, therefore, been 'humbled'. The girls' father has been disabled by a nervous disease. A big man, he sways and stumbles, burning his hand when he tries to put coal on the fire. The third sister, Bertha, takes charge of him and of the baby.

Mr Kendal the clergyman arrives on his bicycle. A tall, thin and ugly bachelor, to whom women are 'unliving, Biblical things', he is afraid of this family. He treats Hilda with great respect during tea. The christening follows at the tea-table, the child being named Joseph William after his grandfather. Emma sees her brother Laurie, black from the pit, grinning sarcastically at her through the window. Mr Rowbotham prays aloud, blaming himself for the shortcomings of his children. He has stood between them and God: better, he says, for this child to have no earthly father.

Washing in the kitchen, Laurie is filled with shame and fear as he listens to his father. He grins, however, when he sees the cake-bag because the child's father is Berryman's assistant. The prayers end. Laurie sings a rhyme to the child, its words mocking his sister who strikes at him. Their father sits, unconcerned. His will-power still controls all his children, who are only 'half-individuals'.

NOTES AND GLOSSARY:

British School:	a school maintained by the British and Foreign Schools Society, a Nonconformist association

macaroons:	sweet biscuits made of almonds
nöwt:	(*dialect*) nothing
locomotor ataxy:	a disease of the nervous system which affects control of the muscles
deacon:	in a Nonconformist chapel, a lay official
voile:	semi-transparent material
murmuring:	complaining
a willow-tree:	see the Bible, Ezekiel 17:5
Blortin':	(*dialect*) blurting
a lodestone:	an iron magnet
The daisies . . . morning:	note the biblical style here; compare Psalm 98:8

'Daughters of the Vicar'

Section I

The Reverend Ernest Lindley is Vicar of Aldecross. This village has a new church intended for the colliers. The coming of the mines has transformed the district. Mr Lindley has been at Cambridge University, and his wife is the daughter of a prosperous Cambridgeshire rector. The colliers and their wives are quite unimpressed by these distinctions. They mostly disregard him, or treat him with contempt. The majority attend Nonconformist chapels, not the Church of England. He begins to hate the local people. He is poor, socially isolated and unhappy. His wife grows sullen. The children are brought up in genteel poverty, completely apart from the mining community; they are taught to be proud of their status. Miss Mary, the eldest, is handsome and tall; she looks proud and pure. Miss Louisa, next in age, is 'short and plump and obstinate-looking'. Grown-up, the girls earn a little money from private lessons.

Section II

One day when Mary is 'about twenty', Mr Lindley visits the Durants of Quarry Cottage, parishioners who keep a haberdasher's shop. Mrs Durant is unhappy because her youngest son, Alfred, has joined the Navy. The Vicar says this is a fine, honourable life, but she thinks that he has gone off to make 'a slave' of himself when he is needed at home. The Lindley family agree that Alfred has recently been getting into idle, drunken ways: the Navy will teach him discipline. Louisa is sorry because she remembers 'a laughing, warm lad, with . . . something rich about him'. She will miss Alfred.

Section III

Three years later, Mr Lindley falls ill, and the Reverend Mr Massy comes to officiate for three months in his place. When the family first hear of him he seems an ideal husband for one of the girls: a young man who has recently won distinctions at Oxford, who has private means, and a church in Northamptonshire to go on to, with a good stipend. They are disappointed when he arrives: he is a tiny, timid man, who looks like 'a little abortion' and seems to lack the full range of human feelings. He is all intellect. Twenty-three years of poverty have ground away Mrs Lindley's pride, however, and she welcomes him because he is rich and respectable.

Mr Massy works hard. He acts as a good Christian, although his religion is founded on logic rather than feeling. Mary respects him for his work and helps him in the parish, overhearing the people laughing at the 'sickly little shrimp'. Louisa cannot bear him. Visiting the dying Mr Durant, she thinks of Mr Massy as an 'inhuman being'. She is impressed, on the other hand, by the sun-tanned, handsome Alfred, now home again.

Section IV

Mr Durant dies. Louisa is unhappy because Alfred has become stiff and distant, as though he ranked himself below her. She tells herself that Alfred is a coward, but in her heart she holds on to him.

Section V

Six months later, Mary marries Mr Massy. Her mother approves of the match. Louisa is furious. Mary tells herself that she has overcome and sacrificed her body in order to 'buy' a superior social position. She will henceforth devote herself to charity and 'high-minded living'. She suffers when she sees how people are repelled by her husband. She will not let herself hate him, sheltering in her pride. Mr Massy is a kind and just husband. When a son, Jack, is born, the father becomes obsessed with his well-being. With her baby, Mary finds that she has not overcome her body, after all, and she feels lost.

Section VI

Louisa feels isolated. She still loves her sister, but believes that Mary is 'degraded in the body'.

Section VII

Three years later, Mary gives birth to a daughter. She persuades Mr Massy to spend Christmas with her parents. They set off for the vicarage by train, a journey which serves to show just how exacting a parent Mr Massy has become. Mr Lindley is now a grey, pitiful figure. Jack disregards his father, who continues to fuss over both children. 'Sullenly angry', Louisa goes out of the house.

Section VIII

Louisa walks through the snow to call on Mrs Durant. Finding her among the cabbages in the garden, injured by a fall, Louisa sends for the doctor, and puts the old woman to bed. Mrs Durant frets about Alfred's dinner. She has not told him about the tumour which has long troubled her. Sexually inexperienced, Alfred is 'not free' of his mother: he feels inadequate, 'not a man'. The Navy has not helped him to mature.

Section IX

Alfred has returned to the pit where he worked before joining the Navy. The men like and admire him. He hides his feelings of inadequacy, enjoying comradeship at work and the contrast between the dark world underground and the changing seasons above.

Section X

Alfred's delight in the snow ends when he finds Louisa at home, and learns of his mother's illness. Louisa serves his dinner, gazing at his face masked by coal dust. The old woman knows that she is dying, but insists that Alfred be helped to wash. He always wants his back washing. Filled with tenderness, Louisa washes his back. It is only when he is fully dressed again that she sees him as a workman. She hates to see him behaving in a deferential way towards her. He feels a little afraid of her.

Section XI

The grandeur of the vicarage, where Alfred reports to the Durants that Louisa is to spend the night caring for his mother, humbles him. Looking at the constellation of the Plough, as he walks home, he grieves for his mother. At six in the morning he asks, should he go to work? He feels despair when his mother tells him to go, but he obeys her wish nonetheless.

Section XII

Word reaches him, as he leaves the pit-mouth, that his mother has died. Mary invites him to the vicarage next Sunday, but he feels socially out of place there, and thinks of emigrating to Canada.

Section XIII

Two evenings later, Louisa goes to Quarry Cottage. She and Alfred talk awkwardly. She asks if he wants her to leave. Although tormented by conflicting emotions, he embraces her. Her blouse is smudged by his coal-dust.

Section XIV

Alfred takes her home. She kisses him and tells him to come to ask her father tomorrow for permission to marry her. He is still troubled by grief for his mother, but he feels he has won a victory: 'something was sound in his heart'.

Section XV

Alfred speaks to the vicar. The Lindleys are worried about the social embarrassment the marriage will involve. It is agreed that when Louisa and Alfred are married they will emigrate to Canada. Humbly, Louisa asks Alfred not to mind her family.

NOTES AND GLOSSARY:

throng:	(*dialect*) busy
Chapel:	Nonconformist Protestants (Methodists, Baptists or Congregationalists) rather than Church of England, which, except in the rural parishes, was considered middle-class
wideawake:	a broad-brimmed soft felt hat
almanacs:	calendars of the year's events
tundish:	(*dialect*) funnel
shall yer put it down:	will you put it on account?
John Wesley:	(1703–91) preacher and hymn-writer, founder of Methodism
John Milton:	(1608–74) poet, author of the epic *Paradise Lost* (1667), and greatest Puritan thinker
Roman Law:	an improbable subject for a future clergyman, chosen because it sounds dry
***chétif*:**	(*French*) puny
stertorous:	with a snoring sound

swaled away:	(*dialect*) melted away
Fabians:	the Fabian Society, founded in 1884, aimed to achieve a socialist society by gradual stages of reforms
snap-bag:	to carry snap, food to be eaten at work
panchion:	earthenware bowl
fritter:	(*dialect*) fragments
registrar:	keeper of official records, including those of marriages; Louisa and Alfred choose a secular marriage, rather than one in church

'Tickets, Please'

It is wartime, and the trams which run through the industrial country-side, in and out of the Midland town, are driven by men physically unfit for military service, and therefore possessed by the spirit of the devil. It is an adventure to ride on these trams. The conductors are all strong fearless girls, who stand for no nonsense, however over-crowded the decks become at busy times. In the mornings when passengers are fewer, soft romance is permitted if good-looking inspectors come aboard. The chief inspector is John Thomas Raynor, known as John Thomas or Coddy. He flirts with the girls in the mornings and walks out with them at night.

Annie is a sharp-tongued conductress who keeps John Thomas at bay, watching him make conquests among the other girls. One night she meets him at the Statutes fair and he gallantly treats her to the roundabouts, winning hat-pins for her at quoits. Later, he cuddles her skilfully in the darkness of the cinema. She walks out with him, keeping her boy-friend 'dangling'. But when she wants 'to take an intelligent interest in him' as a person, not just a sensual 'nocturnal presence', he drops her at once. She is furious and wretched. Then she goes to talk to Nora Purdy, whom John Thomas has taken out in the past. She talks to his other old flames too.

After a while, John Thomas casts an eye on Annie once again, and they make a rendezvous at the depot at a quarter to ten at night. On arrival, he finds waiting the six girls who know him best. They say he must choose one of them – the one he wants to marry. He is reluctant to choose. They push him against the wall and tell him that he must not look to see who is touching him. Annie boxes his ears and knocks off his cap, and they all fly at him, slapping and punching, in fun at first. He tries to escape, but the door is locked. 'Choose!' they cry. Possessed by 'a terrifying lust', Annie hits him with her belt. The girls all tear at his clothes, beating, punching and forcing him to the ground, where he lies like a captive animal. Annie cries out that he ought to be killed. He must choose! He chooses her. This breaks the spell.

Annie is appalled. Each of the other girls hopes he will look at her; but he picks up the shreds of his uniform and, when they unlock the door, leaves. Nora yells his rude nickname, 'Coddy'. As if in torture, Annie tells her to 'shut up'. The other girls have 'mute stupefied faces'.

NOTES AND GLOSSARY:

Trams that pass in the night: in *Tales of a Wayside Inn*, H. W. Longfellow (1807–82) compares 'Ships that pass in the night' to our passage 'on the ocean of life'

sang-froid: (*French*) coolness, composure

antiphony: in church music, the alternate singing of verses of a psalm or canticle by two sections of the choir

Thermopylae: the action of Leonidas and three hundred Spartans in fighting to the death in 480BC to hold the pass of this name (which means 'The Hot Gates' in Greek) against a Persian army which vastly outnumbered them has always been regarded as an example of supreme courage and self-sacrifice

John Thomas, Coddy: slang term for the penis

a Tartar: as fierce as Tartars were reputed to be

Statutes fair: held every November at Eastwood, when Lawrence was young; the name confirms our impression that the county town is Nottingham

naphtha: inflammable oil

pastures new: 'At last he rose, and twitch'd his mantle blue;/ Tomorrow to fresh woods, and pastures new.' John Milton, 'Lycidas' (1637)

qui vive: (*French*) the challenge of a sentry, 'Who goes there?', hence alertness

toddling: going

'You Touched Me'

Ted Rockley is dying of a kidney disease. He is a rich man, owner of the Pottery House, an ugly brick building next to the old pottery, no longer in use. He has four daughters: two are married; Matilda and Emmie are still at home. They will inherit ten thousand pounds each. There are no respectable husbands to be found, however, and sooner than marry beneath their own class, they prefer to grow into old maids. Matilda is tall, graceful and artistic. Emmie is short, plump and a good housekeeper.

Sixteen years ago, tired of an exclusively female household, Ted adopted a six-year-old orphan, Hadrian. All attempts to educate this boy as a young gentleman failed. Hadrian remained stubbornly Cockney, impudent and lawless. At fifteen, he went to Canada to become an electrician. The First World War brought him back to Europe as a soldier, and now the war is over he has come to the Pottery House again.

The girls suspect his motives, but Ted tells them that Hadrian's name is not in the will: Ted's watch and chain, and a hundred pounds to take back to Canada, are all he is to inherit. Hadrian does not want to stay in England, because he hates 'the difference' between masters and men. Nonetheless, he would like to be a master.

Pitying her father, Matilda goes to his room one night, and lays her hand, as she thinks, on his brow; but the man in the bed is Hadrian – her father, she remembers too late, is sleeping downstairs. Her hand aches from the contact. She dislikes Hadrian and fears him, knowing him to be unscrupulous. He is surprised by 'the fragile sensitiveness of her caress': there is a 'high-bred sensitiveness' about Matilda, he thinks, akin to the quality he admires in her father. Wanting to be master of it, he asks Ted if he can marry Matilda. Ted likes the idea, and tells Matilda that he will disinherit her and her sister unless she marries Hadrian. A new will is drawn up making the girls' inheritance dependent on Matilda's marrying Hadrian.

Hadrian wants the money because he wants to own his own business, but he wants Matilda too. When the girls accuse him of scheming for the money, he insists that he wants Matilda for herself. He tells her that she is committed to him because 'You touched me'. She feels trapped. She tells her father she will marry Hadrian. They marry three days later. She kisses her father, for the first time since childhood, and, at his command, kisses Hadrian: ' "That's right! That's right!" murmured the dying man.'

NOTES AND GLOSSARY:

drays: low carts without sides

Mary . . . Martha: Mary chose higher things, while Martha was a good housekeeper. See the Bible, Luke 10:38–42

a Charity Institution: an orphanage

dropsy: disease which produces an excess of watery fluid in the body

the Armistice: the Armistice which ended the First World War was signed on 11 November 1918

You wouldn't make a life-guardsman: Hadrian is short
sotto voce: (*Italian*) in a low voice
confab: confabulation, discussion
plebeian: the *plebs* were the lowest class in ancient Roman society, hence lower-class; here, with the connotation of vulgar
sliving: (*dialect*) slippery

'Fanny and Annie'

Fanny, a lady's maid, has come home to the town in the Midlands where, twelve years ago, she became engaged to Harry Goodall, a foundry-worker. She has been keeping him 'dangling' all this time. He meets her train. The station is near the furnaces where he works, and when she sees him his face is lit by the flames. He has no collar; and rather than take a cab, he carries her cases. She disapproves, contrasting her present situation with what she has been used to – her mistress's carriage meeting the train at Gloucester, and everyone polite, even to the maid. What a come-down!

Fanny stays with her Aunt Lizzie, who keeps a sweet-shop. The aunt admires and feels sorry for Fanny, so beautiful and ladylike and proud. Harry is not good enough for her. A woman's voice calls from the street, just as Harry is delivering Fanny's trunk on a cart, threatening to 'shame' him. Harry is thirty-two, fair, and attractive to women. He has no obvious vices. Fanny regrets his lack of ambition and initiative.

Mrs Goodall is a large, obstinate woman who hates correct English and anything else that she regards as pretentiousness. She admires Fanny rather grudgingly, and respects her because her Aunt Kate has left her two hundred pounds. The wedding is to be in two weeks' time, at Morley Chapel, where Harry is in the choir. He has a good voice, but cannot manage aitches, singing 'Hangels . . . hever bright an' fair', and also 'dropping' them. Next Sunday is Harvest Festival and Harry is to sing solo. Fanny remembers a Harvest Festival ten years ago which she attended with her cousin Luther, a student from London, far more clever than Harry. Looking at Harry in the chapel, she is divided between strong physical attraction and a sense that he drags her down.

Harry's singing is interrupted by shouts from a red-faced woman in the congregation. This is Mrs Nixon, known as 'a devil' who beats her drunken husband and her lanky grown-up daughters. She accuses Harry of 'refusing to take the consequences'. The minister, Mr Enderby, gives out the last hymn and order is restored. 'Most unfortunate', says Mr Enderby afterwards. Harry explains that

Annie Nixon, one of the daughters, is pregnant, but that is no more likely to be his fault than 'some other chap's', because Annie is always with the fellows. Mr Enderby decides that Harry, although a sinner, can remain a member of the choir.

Back at Mrs Goodall's for tea, Fanny is slow to decide whether or not she too can forgive him. The family agree that Mrs Nixon is a dreadful shrew. Harry is going back to the chapel to sing in the evening service. Fanny says the decisive word to Mrs Goodall: 'I'm not going tonight. . . . I'll stop with *you* tonight, mother'.

NOTES AND GLOSSARY:

chatelaine:	a string of beads at the waist to hold keys, etc
ormin':	(*dialect*) gormless, stupid
I towd him . . . bargain:	(*dialect*) I told him myself. She has held back all this time; let her stay as she is [unmarried]. He [Harry] would not have agreed to marry you if he had listened to me, do you hear? No, he is a fool, and I know it. I say to him, 'A fine man you look at your age going and opening the door to her when you hear her at the gate, after she has finished her gallivanting. You look a rare softy.' But it's no use talking: he answered your letter and made his own bad bargain
Baalam's ass:	the ass refused to carry Baalam past the angel, despite being beaten. See the Bible, Numbers 22:21–35
vernacular:	in this instance, it means dialect
Lot's wife:	she was turned to a pillar of salt. See the Bible, Genesis 19:26
washed his hands:	Pilate washed his hands to show that he disclaimed responsibility for Christ's death. See the Bible, Matthew 27:24
a tanger:	(*dialect*) a terror

'Monkey Nuts'

The First World War is recently over, and two soldiers, Albert, a middle-aged corporal, and young Joe, are billeted in a country cottage and working at a railway station. One of the 'land-girls' recruited during the war comes to the station with hay-wagons. She calls herself Miss Stokes. She finds Joe attractive, but he has little to say to her. Albert jokes with her but to no avail. One Saturday she sends a telegram signed M.S., making a date with Joe, but he spends the evening with Albert as usual. When Joe shows him the telegram, Albert talks of the artfulness of women.

A circus is coming to the district. Albert invites Miss Stokes to go with the two of them, but offers to stay at home when Joe blurts out that his presence would be 'too many be half'. Albert says Joe wants to know what 'M.S.' stands for. 'Monkey nuts', she jeers. Joe is embarrassed and angry.

At the circus, Joe notices Miss Stokes, who is pretending not to see him. He and Albert meet her on the way home. Her bicycle has a puncture. Joe is afraid of her. Albert flirts with her. She takes Joe's hand, mortifying him. She asks Albert to put her bicycle away while Joe walks her home. Joe refuses. 'She bain't my choice.' Miss Stokes puts her arm round his waist. Albert leaves them together. Walking with her, Joe feels 'maddened, but helpless'. Nonetheless, he begins to go out regularly with Miss Stokes, whom Albert, who does not treat the relationship seriously, persists in calling 'Monkey nuts'. Joe grows sullen and irritable. One night Albert orders Joe to say what is wrong. Joe says he does not want the girl but cannot break free.

Next day Albert goes to meet Miss Stokes in place of Joe. Speaking in the facetious manner he always uses, he says that Joe did not want to come and proposes that she take him as a lover; his banter is silenced when she bursts into tears. Afterwards, he tells Joe he is better off without Monkey nuts. When Miss Stokes brings her wagon in the morning, she beckons Joe to join her. He is about to obey when Albert stops him: 'Work's work, and nuts is nuts.' He puts a hand on Joe's shoulder. Miss Stokes calls to Joe, but he jeers at her, 'Monkey nuts!' She whitens with rage. After that, she no longer comes with the hay. Joe feels more relaxed than he felt when the war ended.

NOTES AND GLOSSARY:

Flanders:	battleground of the First World War
ennui:	weary discontent
land-girls:	women recruited to work on farms and so free farm-workers for military service
grid:	grid-iron, that is the bicycle
She bain't:	(*dialect*) she isn't
puttees:	bands of cloth wound round the lower leg, as part of military uniform
mettle:	pun on mettle (spirit) and metal
Gilbert . . . nuts:	in this context a nut (or knut) is a 'swell' or young man about town. In Basil Hallam's early twentieth-century popular song, Gilbert the Filbert was 'Colonel of the K-nuts'

Am I my brother's keeper?: Cain's words to God about Abel. See the
Bible, Genesis 4:9

beans: (*slang of the period*) trouble

armistice: see notes and glossary to 'You Touched Me'

'The Rocking-Horse Winner'

Paul, aged about twelve, has always felt that his mother does not love
him enough because she is worried about money. His mother grew up
accustomed to luxury, in a rich upper-class family, and married for
love, although the love did not last, a man of her own social
background but without a good enough income to support the 'style'
in which they live. Paul and his sisters can always hear their house
whispering, '*There must be more money! There must be more money!*'
Nobody ever says the words aloud, but the whisper is everywhere.

Paul asks his mother (born Cresswell; her Christian and married
names are not given) why they do not have their own car but always
use Uncle Oscar's or a taxi. She says his father has no luck. Luck is
what causes you to have money. She used to be lucky, before she
married. Paul declares that he is a lucky person. God has told him so.
His mother is unimpressed and this annoys him: he wants to win her
attention.

He takes to riding his big wooden rocking-horse, because 'he *knew*
the horse could take him to where there was luck'. He rides furiously
and his big blue eyes glare with determination. Uncle Oscar asks the
horse's name. The name changes, says Paul. Last week he was
Sansovino. Oscar is interested in that, because Sansovino won at
Ascot. Paul's mother tells her brother that Paul discusses horse-
racing with Bassett, the gardener. Oscar takes Paul for a ride in the
car and questions him. Paul says he and Bassett are partners; he
started winning on races when he bet the ten shillings his uncle gave
him. Paul means to bet three hundred pounds on Daffodil to win the
Lincoln, but this is a secret. Bassett looks after the money; he is more
cautious and keeps a larger reserve. Oscar takes his nephew to the
Lincoln races. Daffodil wins at odds of four to one. Bassett convinces
Oscar that Paul is telling the truth. Paul now has fifteen hundred
pounds. Sometimes, Paul says, he is *sure* which horse will win.

Oscar joins the partnership. Paul wins ten thousand pounds on
Lively Spark, an outsider he is *sure* about, in the St Leger. Uncle
Oscar wins two thousand, but feels nervous about betting on this
scale. Paul does not want his mother to know because she would stop
him, but he wants her to have the money. Oscar arranges this through
a lawyer. Paul's mother begins to spend recklessly and the house
intensifies its whispering, terrifying Paul who grows 'wild-eyed and

strange'. He is not sure who the winner of the Grand National will be. He must be sure about the Derby.

Paul's secret is the rocking-horse. He rides himself into a frenzy in which he 'learns' the name of the winner. One night his mother goes to his room and finds him riding frantically. He falls from the horse, calling out 'Malabar', then sinks into a coma for three days. Oscar passes the tip to Bassett. Paul wakes when Bassett is allowed into the bedroom with news about the Derby. Malabar has won him over seventy thousand pounds. Paul boasts to his mother that he *is* lucky; but he dies that night. Oscar Cresswell thinks the boy is 'best gone out of a life where he rides his rocking-horse to find a winner'.

NOTES AND GLOSSARY:

a small income:	small by the standards of the rich
school:	a fee-paying boarding school
Filthy lucre:	sordid financial gain
Ascot:	Royal Ascot, a four-day meeting in June. The Gold Cup is the principal long-distance race of the English flat-racing season
batman:	a soldier who acts as an officer's servant
blade of the 'turf':	keen backer of race-horses
events:	here, races
Nat Gould:	a famous follower of horse-racing, editor of *The Sporting Annual*
Turf Commission:	a mistake for 'Commissioner' (sometimes 'Turf Accountant'); Lawrence meant a book-maker
Leger:	the St Leger, run at Doncaster in September
writs:	summonses for non-payment of debt
Grand National:	the principal steeple-chasing event in England, held at Aintree in late March
Lincolnshire:	the Lincolnshire Handicap, now run at Doncaster, near the end of March
Derby:	the Derby Stakes is run at Epsom on the first Wednesday in June
Eton:	the age for starting at Eton College would have been thirteen. Some of the dialogue makes Paul seem younger, as he is (played by John Howard Davies) in Anthony Pelissier's film (Rank, 1949)

'The Man Who Loved Islands'

Section I

The man wants to own an island in order to create a world of his own. He buys an island and a neighbouring islet (in what appear to be the

Channel Islands), and is happy, feeling united with nature, although he is alarmed by dreams of the island's violent Roman, Saxon and Viking past. Hoping to create an ideal Happy Isle, he spends money restoring the big house. He hires staff: a bailiff, two farm hands, a skipper for his yacht, a carpenter and a mason, with their families; and a butler and a buxom housekeeper. He becomes 'the Master', fawned on and flattered by 'his people'. Bills come in for thousands of pounds, but, he believes, economy among the islanders will set all to rights, and he tells them so. He reads books on farming, and explains his plans to the bailiff, who listens sceptically. The next harvest is celebrated with a harvest-home supper. The Master makes a speech: his theme is true happiness for all, under his rule.

Things go wrong in many ways. A cow falls off a cliff. Pigs become diseased. People quarrel. Violent feelings arise that seem to stem from the island's gory history. The people begin to leave. The bills become ever higher. The Master does not like to face the fact that his 'people' have swindled him. The farm goes on losing money. The island, for all its uncanny beauty, is now his implacable enemy. In his fifth year of ownership, he sells the main island to a hotel company, which plans to turn it into a honeymoon-and-golf island. This will serve the island right!

Section II: 'The Second Island'

The islander moves to his islet, taking only the faithful carpenter (helped by an orphan lad), and a widow and daughter, as retainers. He transfers his books to the more modest house on this rock in the sea. Nevertheless, he feels, it is still an island.

He continues to work on his books about flowers of the ancient world. The islet is peaceful. There are none of the ghosts of the violent past which haunted the first island; the elements have washed away history here. The feudal title of 'The Master' is abandoned and the man is known instead as 'Mr Cathcart'.

Sometimes he goes to London to stay at his club and talk to his publishers, but he is always glad to get back to the islet. He starts to study its flora, and to get to know the widow's daughter, who is called Flora. Almost unwillingly, he makes love to her. This brings no happiness; instead it makes his isle seem 'smirched and spoiled'. He leaves in order to travel in Europe, until Flora writes to say that she is going to have a child.

He buys another islet in the distant northern seas (presumably the Hebrides). He marries Flora, because that is his duty. The southern island is now 'hateful', 'a suburb'. A daughter is born. He leaves Flora money and flees north.

Section III: 'The Third Island'

There is a simple house on the third island. Half a dozen sheep graze and a cat keeps him company. He has lost interest in his book. He wants no ships or boats to come. Starting to loathe the sheep, he has them removed. He can tolerate the sea and the sea-gulls, but he dislikes visits from fishermen. He ignores the letters they bring, but still dresses neatly. When winter all but wipes out daylight, he sinks into mental lethargy. Storms are good times for him, he feels, because they isolate the island. His cat disappears.

Snow falls, and walls him in. He digs himself out to get at his boat, but gradually the snow defeats him. You cannot win, he tells himself, against the elements. Now he lives only with sea and snow and wind.

NOTES AND GLOSSARY:

Abraham:	God promised Abraham to 'multiply [his] seed as the stars of the heaven, and as the sand which is upon the sea shore'. See the Bible, Genesis 22:17
spats:	cloth gaiters, buttoned round the ankles
men of Gaul:	invaders from France, known as Gaul in the Roman Empire
priests with a crucifix:	Christian missionaries in Anglo-Saxon times
pirates:	Vikings
Hesperides:	in Greek mythology, three sisters who guarded a tree with golden apples in the Islands of the Blest, a paradise at the western-most end of the earth
Hermes:	herald, messenger and herdsman to the ancient Greek gods
lean kine:	see the Bible, Genesis 41. Pharaoh's dream warned of seven lean years
Orion:	a constellation of stars, pictured as a hunter with dogs and animals
Flora:	the name of the Roman goddess of flowers; 'the flora' are the flowers of a region
Golders Green:	a London suburb

'Things'

Erasmus and Valerie Melville, he from Connecticut, she from Massachusetts, marry, some years before the First World War, and settle in Paris to enjoy civilised freedom on a private income, modest but sufficient for Americans in Europe, of three thousand dollars a year. They are a high-minded couple, idealists, interested in Buddhism, lovers of art and architecture, people who yearn for 'a full and beautiful life'. Paris offers this, for some years. But it seems to them that human freedom is not feasible without support: 'human beings are all vines'. Simply living in Paris disappoints after a time; the Melvilles feel that the French are too materialistic; and they move to Italy, when the war begins.

Italy delights them. It is more like New England in its pure beauty, and, being less cynical than France, it is a suitable place for practising Buddhism. The idealists dream of a perfect world, seeking by meditation to eliminate greed, pain and sorrow from their souls. The war upsets them. When America becomes involved, they do hospital work, which teaches them to doubt whether even Buddhism can eliminate greed, pain and sorrow from the world. They are vines which slide off the pole of 'Indian thought'.

They still have Italy, their 'freedom' (as they call financial independence), 'beauty' and, now, a child, Peter, whom they are too wise to 'fasten upon'. But Europe has finally disappointed them. Although lovely, Europe is dead, materialistic, lacking soul, a place of mere survivors.

Meanwhile the idealists have their lovely house, overlooking the river Arno, filled with the furniture and other beautiful 'things' they have been picking up ever since they arrived in Europe. But even the beauty of the 'things', satisfying as it is when people praise their home, is finally not enough in itself, and 'for the boy's sake' they decide to return to materialistic America.

They reach America with several van-loads of 'things', but their income only pays for a small apartment in New York: the 'things' go into a warehouse. Erasmus could easily get a university job, but that would be a sacrifice of freedom. They try to live out West, but find they are enslaved there by 'chores'. A millionaire friend offers them a house full of labour-saving devices in California where they are convinced that there will be opportunities for renewing the soul, but after a year California, too, disappoints.

Meanwhile the cost of keeping the 'things' in store (six hundred dollars a year) has become financially crippling. They end their journey at Cleveland University, where Erasmus is persuaded to accept a professorship. Their house on campus is admired by all for its beautiful 'things', and Valerie is happy with them. But Erasmus ('Dick' to his wife) now know that he is a materialist; he has rat-like eyes: he feels he is in the cage. Although he is materially satisfied, he is cursed with 'a queer, evil scholastic look of pure scepticism'.

NOTES AND GLOSSARY:

Connecticut . . . Massachusetts: these are among the six north-eastern states of the USA, known since the seventeenth century as New England

Mrs Besant: Annie Besant (1847–1933), one of the founders of the Theosophical Society (1875). See below for a note on Theosophy

baroque: a style of architecture, exuberantly ornamented, which flourished in the seventeenth and eighteenth centuries. The term also applies to some of the art, music and literature of that period

Renaissance: (*French*) rebirth. The term applies to all new developments in arts and sciences in Europe in the fifteenth and sixteenth centuries

New Haven: a town in Connecticut

Boulevard Montparnasse: a tree-lined street in Paris

Monet: Claude Monet (1840–1926), French landscape artist, a leader of the nineteenth-century Impressionist school of painters, who aimed to catch the impressions ('shimmer') of colour and movement in nature

Montmartre: a district in Paris famous for its steep streets, its night-life and its artists

Tuileries: gardens and walks in the centre of Paris

boulevards: main streets, full of life in the evenings

materialism: in philosophy, the denial of the spiritual; generally, excessive concern with possessions

Buddha: (*Sanskrit*) the Enlightened. The title of Gautama, fifth-century BC founder of Buddhism, a religion fashionable among Western intellectuals in Lawrence's time. The Buddha taught that the soul, until purified, is tied to material things

America . . . war: America entered the First World War in 1917

theosophy: claiming secret knowledge of the nature of things, Theosophists taught that human beings have latent powers. A vague, contemplative religious system, Theosophy was also known as Esoteric Buddhism

Nirvana: Buddhists believe that the soul is freed from the pain of material existence in the final state of Nirvana

bho tree: the Buddha sat beneath one for seven days while struggling with temptation

Seitzfleisch: (*German*, correctly *Sitzfleisch*) literally seat-flesh, so steadiness, or, here, ability to sit still

New Englanders: Lawrence was thinking of the region's Puritan, idealist traditions

beanstalk . . . Jill: Jack climbs a beanstalk to the sky, in the fairy-story; Jack and Jill fall down the hill, in the nursery rhyme

palazzo: (*Italian*) palace or big town-house

Arno: the river on which Florence is built

salotto: (*Italian*) sitting-room

Chartres: a cathedral near Paris; its sculptures and stained glass represent to Valerie the keenest aesthetic experience, tinged with spirituality

Ark of the Covenant: a wooden coffer containing the stone tablets inscribed with the Ten Commandments. It was 'the Holy of Holies' or innermost shrine in the Temple of Solomon. The Philistines were punished by God when they opened it. See the Bible, I Samuel 4–6

ad infinitum: (*Latin*) indefinitely

anathema: an accursed thing

Sodom and Gomorrah: the Cities of the Plain, destroyed by God because of the wickedness of their inhabitants. See the Bible, Genesis 19

A scholastic career: as a teacher in a university

Yale: the university is in New Haven

Cleveland University: in Ohio

Louis-Quinze: of the period of the eighteenth-century French king Louis XV

Part 3

Commentary

Nature, purpose and achievement

Lawrence wanted his stories to be absorbing and accurate, sad or amusing, because he wanted them to be true to life, or, in his phrase, 'on the side of life'. Friends, neighbours and workmates are usually in the background ('Strike-Pay' is an exception). In the foreground are parents and children, lovers and suitors, husbands and wives. Fulfilment in marriage and family life is always threatened or thwarted: money, false ideas about social status, and false culture distract people from the true claims of life. Lawrence brought to this traditional, moral approach to personal relations a vision of unusual intensity. Parenthood, love and marriage are always, in Lawrence's work, extremely difficult. They are battles to be fought at great cost, glorious in victory, dreadful in defeat – and unavoidable. The man who evades them will end on a rock in the sea, hating everyone. These are life's demands and they unleash instinctive, violent forces deep within us, mysterious and only to be expressed in metaphors. Lawrence believed that most previous fiction was inadequate because writers underestimated or ignored these forces. In essays and novels he used strong terms and impassioned rhetoric to try to convey his beliefs. He is most persuasive in his short stories, as in his novels, when his fiction makes us look at life the way he wanted.

'Odour of Chrysanthemums' tells of a wife who learns that she has failed her husband only when he is killed; 'Strike-Pay' ends with a husband and wife united in spite of the power of money; 'The Christening' contains a father who has crushed the life out of his children – and a typically Lawrentian attack on 'respectability'; one sister in 'Daughters of the Vicar' chooses respectability and denies life, while the second is braver, and so is able to help a son, too possessively loved, to break free of his mother. These stories belong to the first stage of Lawrence's story writing. Denial or acceptance of life is the theme they share.

In **'Odour of Chrysanthemums'** (first published in 1911; revised 1914), Lawrence conveys the shock and pathos of the sudden death of a miner, a father of young children, and although this was not his main purpose, it contributes to the quality of the story. Walter's workmates wonder at the seemingly expert fashion in which the mine has killed him.

"E wor under th' face, an' it niver touched 'im. It shut 'im in. It seems 'e wor smothered.' . . .

"Sphyxiated . . . Seems as if it was done o' purpose. Clean over him, an' shut 'im in . . .'

The men downstairs can hear Annie's frightened voice in the bedroom, asking if her father is home and if he is drunk, and they flee from it: 'None of them spoke till they were far away from the wakeful children.'

The heart of the story is Elizabeth's realisation that she shares with her husband the blame for the failure of her marriage. She decides that although she has borne their children, she has never known or loved Walter. Instead, she has formed a simplified picture of him as a drunk and spendthrift, which has kept her from the real man. She begins to imagine his mind and feelings only now that these are gone.

And he . . . how awful he must have felt it to be a husband. She felt that in the next world he would be a stranger to her. If they met there, in the beyond, they would only be ashamed of what had been before . . . They had denied each other in life. Now he had withdrawn. An anguish came over her . . . he had been her husband. But how little!

She suffers because life is not to be denied.

Lawrence brings his idea to life by showing Elizabeth's isolation. She assumes that Walter is out drinking and nurses her wrath until her bitterness encloses her. Her father arrives in his railway engine, asking for a cup of tea 'in a cheery, hearty fashion', which she swiftly dispels; a 'dangerous coldness' enters his voice, and he is soon moralising over Walter's making 'a beast of himself' in the 'Lord Nelson'. Her anger subdues her children, who play 'united in fear'. Mr and Mrs Rigley are helpful and polite, but their voices are 'tinged with respect': Elizabeth's educated, standard English distances her from the warmth of their dialect. Her mother-in-law is not thinking of Elizabeth's worries but remembering Walter as a merry boy, and reflecting that you have to 'make allowances' for male weakness. The children and their grandmother love Walter, and the neighbours accept him in spite of his weakness. Elizabeth seems cold in contrast, by the time her self-discovery comes.

The two 'masters' referred to in the last two sentences of the story – life and death – are symbolised in the flowers. They are associated at first with the children. Elizabeth plucks and smells the spray of chrysanthemums in a moment of pity for John. The sight of them in her mother's apron gives Annie 'a little rapture'. Then they and their odour are linked with Elizabeth's bitterness.

'Don't they smell beautiful!'
Her mother gave a short laugh.
'No,' she said, 'not to me. It was chrysanthemums when I married him, and chrysanthemums when you were born, and the first time they ever brought him home drunk, he'd got brown chrysanthemums in his button-hole.'

After the first collier has been with the news, Elizabeth senses the 'cold, deathly smell' of the pink chrysanthemums standing in two vases. The stretcher-bearing collier knocks the vase off just as the coat falls, exposing the half-naked body 'stripped for work', and Elizabeth rushes to mop up sooner than look. Three pages later when she feels 'the child within her [as] a weight apart from her', we should remember how Annie put her face to the flowers at her mother's waist, admiring them as flowers of life, and souvenirs of her birth. Now they are funeral flowers.

'**Strike-Pay**' (first published in 1913) is attractive in its lightness of touch with a serious subject – what money means to poor people – and in the assertion that, ultimately, money is not what matters most. Ephraim's display of horsemanship on the pit-pony typifies the attractive swagger which the miners assume, although they cannot afford it, for the sake of morale and dignity. Waiting their turn for ten shillings and a bob a kid from the Union agent provokes 'ragging' and gales of laughter. The half-sovereigns 'click' on the bars of the public houses. Skittles and football make the strike seem like a holiday. The scene in the Primitive Methodist Chapel, and the walk to Nottingham, show directly the camaraderie of life in the pit – 'an ease, a go-as-you-please about the day underground' – which Alfred in 'Daughters of the Vicar' is said to enjoy and which first drew him to mining: 'Like the other boys, he had insisted on going into the pit as soon as he left school, because that was the only way speedily to become a man, level with all the other men.' It is unmanly to care overmuch about money: the others 'share' with Ephraim when his half-sovereign cannot be found, and Sam Coutts risks enough, betting on skittles, to win half a crown. He spends some of it at once on a round of drinks and bread and cheese. The women, on the other hand, sit at home, counting the pennies, and sooner or later they have to be faced. The battle of the sexes is presented with humour, in this not quite unhappy ending. The virago of a mother-in-law is not to be taken seriously, and although the mild Ephraim is afraid of her, he defends himself. The workman stifled to death in mud whom he sees on his way home is perhaps meant as a reminder that the workers' cause should not be treated frivolously. If so it is the story's one heavy-handed touch. The contrasting images of Ephraim careering about the field, riding and chasing his pony, and the four men soberly searching the field are far more effective. Equally good is the ending: when the mother-in-law has left shouting 'trollops', Maud makes the forgiving cup of tea because Ephraim is *her* man, not her mother's'. In different ways, the pony-riding and the tea, although one is sheer recklessness and the other is a shade possessive, assert that money is not everything in life.

'The Christening' (first published in 1914) explores a paradox: life can become so egotistical and wilful in a father that it crushes life out of his children. Although locomotor ataxy sends the old miner lurching about his house, falling into the fire, and slavering, he can still dominate, and the last lines of the story are a good setting for one of Lawrence's terms for people in whom life has been thwarted, 'sullen':

> The day after the christening he staggered in at the doorway declaring, in a loud voice, with joy in life still: 'The daisies light up the earth, they clap their hands in multitudes, in praise of the morning.' And his daughters shrank, sullen.

His children have grown up only 'half-individuals'. The story's comments on them illustrate the way the words 'life' and 'live' signify in Lawrence a positive achievement: 'They had never lived; his life, his will had always been upon them and contained them.' The obedience of the 'humbled' Emma is 'to a sensitive observer . . . more intolerable than the most hateful discord', because the hateful discord is buried beneath it. Emma's love for her baby burns in her blood, but she is not allowed to show her feelings.

'A man child is born unto us, therefore let us rejoice and be glad.' The minister's words express Lawrence's view, and the point of the story is that such people cannot rejoice. The minister is afraid of the family. Bertha's pleasure in the baby is mixed with contempt for its mother. The youth Laurie hates his father and jeers at his sisters. Mr Rowbotham contemplates the complete moral and spiritual failure of his children with grim satisfaction: 'For I've been like a stone upon them, and they rise up and curse me in their wickedness.' It is in Hilda that Lawrence offers his explanation of the remarkably joyless atmosphere he has created around the minister's words about the man child. The christening is more wretched for her than for the others because, for her, it is a respectable occasion.

Because Hilda is 'a college-trained schoolmistress', she is obliged to assert and protect her status as a lady, among the disrespectful mining folk. Her 'remarkably rapid and nervous' words to the baker are assertive, and he retaliates, 'How's that sister o' yours getting on?' She replies with 'sharp, ironical defiance'; but the half-mile of the main street is then 'slow-stepping torture' to her, because she feels 'the mark upon the family, against which the common folk could lift their fingers'. The minister, who treats Hilda with great respect, acknowledges that hers is a superior household. Laurie's mocking allusion to the baby's father in 'Pat-a-cake, pat-a-cake, baker's man', and his sister's reaction, make an appropriately nasty climax, meant to convey Lawrence's opinion of this sort of vulgar, lifeless 'respectability'.

'Daughters of the Vicar' (first published in 1914) attacks middle-class respectability of the kind which nineteenth-century novelists called 'shabby-genteel'. It is because Mr Lindley is so poor – by his standards, not the miners' – that he instils in his children a rigid code of social superiority. They are well described in the first section of the story, going into church 'with mute clear faces, childish mouths closed in pride that was like a doom to them, and childish eyes already unseeing'. The way in which pride turns out to be a doom to Mary but not to Louisa is schematic but nonetheless effective. Mr Massy, all intellect, or almost all, seems at first a mere demonstration of Lawrence's theories about the dangers of divorcing mind from body, but he later comes nastily to life in his wilful and ineffectual fussing over his children. Mary's willingness to marry him arises plausibly from her upbringing: as a child she has a 'pure look of submission to a high fate'. Such purity is ominous in Lawrence. Louisa, 'obstinate-looking', sounds healthier.

The scene where Louisa finds herself washing Alfred's back is one of the best of its kind in all Lawrence's fiction. The dying Mrs Durant frets because she cannot do her motherly duty: 'He can't bear if his back isn't washed.' Louisa feels that 'only the suffering woman must be considered', but it hurts her to be 'forced' into their routine:

> Louisa felt the almost repulsive intimacy being forced upon her. It was all so common, so like herding. She lost her own distinctness.

This vicarage-bred distinctness fails to hold her. Habit makes Alfred, who lives so much by instinct, hand back the soap, putting her in his mother's place; washing him, fascinated, Louisa's 'separateness' recedes.

> She had only seen one human being in her life – and that was Mary. All the rest were strangers. Now her soul was going to open, she was going to see another. She felt strange and pregnant.

Such passages succeed in conveying what Lawrence believed about the unity of body and mind. Alfred still has much to suffer before he is 'free' of his mother; Louisa's readiness to 'see' him brings him through. The fact that Louisa and Alfred have to emigrate reflects Lawrence's feeling that England was no longer a good place for those who wanted to shed class and personal distinctness and fulfi themselves in life.

These stories, and most of the others collected in *The Prussiar Officer* (1914), explore situations in ordinary life in the mining communities of the country around Nottingham. Later stories have more varied settings and often more unusual situations. Many pieces in the next collection, *England, My England* (1922), develop Lawrence's idea of sexual relations as a battle. 'Tickets, Please', 'You Touched Me' and 'Monkey Nuts' have the First World War or its immediate aftermath as their background, implying a connection between the war and violence in the sexual natures of men and women. 'Fanny and Annie' is a gentler, comic story, although it too involves as a minor figure a thwarted woman.

'Tickets, Please' (first published in 1919) is often regarded as a miniature modern version of *The Bacchae* by the Greek dramatist Euripides (480–406BC). In this play, Pentheus, king of Thebes, is torn limb from limb by women possessed by the god Dionysus (or Bacchus), whose worship he has tried to suppress. One of the Bacchic women is his mother. The point of comparison is that the conductresses who attack John Thomas are carried away by a force, too strong to resist, which they do not understand and which makes them act with exceptional violence.

> The sight of his white, bare arm maddened the girls. He lay in a kind of trance of fear and antagonism. They felt themselves filled with supernatural strength . . .
>
> 'You ought to be *killed*, that's what you ought,' said Annie, tensely . . . And there was a terrifying lust in her voice.

John Thomas has not offended a god but he has insulted their womanhood. His name implies that he represents crude male lust, unscrupulous in seducing and discarding girls. Like the Bacchic women, the tram-girls are formidable as a group, having their own rites, and their assault on him begins like a ritual game: 'Go on – turn your face to the wall, and don't look, and say which one touches you.' As chief inspector of the trams, John Thomas is a kind of king, and, symbolically, his subjects tear away his uniform. The sight of his flesh stimulates their aggression, mixing it with lust. The supernatural strength of the dark god (or goddess) which rises in the girls sweeps them beyond the bounds of a game or a punishment into a frenzy in which they might kill. Although he is too stunned to think, instinct helps Lawrence's Pentheus.

> He was cunning in his overthrow. He did not give in to them really – no, not if they tore him to bits.
>
> 'All right, then,' he said, 'I choose Annie.'

We may think of Annie as the equivalent to Pentheus's mother, learning too late what she has done. Annie speaks 'as if in torture' at the end. She in her turn has upset the balance of the sexes.

'Tickets, Please' suggests that the First World War was fought, in a sense, in England as well as abroad. The usual drivers have gone away to fight and the unfit men who take their places therefore have 'the spirit of the devil in them', driving the trams like weapons of war, and this spirit infects the conductresses. Annie is used to fighting men off the platform of her tram when it is overcrowded.

She is peremptory, suspicious, and ready to hit first. She can hold her own in ten thousand. The step of that tram-car is her Thermopylae.

Her tram is 'for ever rocking on the waves of a stormy land'. In the wilder spirit which overtakes her at the end, the story implies, there is something akin to the spirit of war. The same forces are active in personal relations and in history, violent and destructive when out of control. The story is successful in keeping its implications, like its analogies to *The Bacchae*, in the background. The final scene is vivid and persuasive. Lawrence knows just how a group of normal girls might attack, and conceivably kill, such a man as Mr Raynor.

The idea of a symbolic, ritual or magic touch links 'Tickets, Please' with **'You Touched Me'** (also first published in 1919). Hadrian returns from the war to conquer Matilda, and wins her when she accidentally touches him. Lawrence suggests here that the physical contact releases instincts thwarted by Matilda's mistaken choice of respectable spinsterhood rather than marriage to a social inferior. If we read the story as he wanted, we sympathise with her fight against social abhorrence of Hadrian; when they kiss at the end we agree with Mr Rockley, who says, 'That's right!' Life has prevailed in spite of the British class system. Nevertheless, the story is difficult to believe. Whatever we may think of Hadrian's impudent Cockney manners, and his mixture of contempt, admiration and envy of the Rockleys' manners, it seems unlikely that Matilda would accept him, even when her father threatens to disinherit her if she does not marry Hadrian. The story is weakened by other improbabilities. Would there be no curates or schoolmasters for the wealthy Miss Rockleys to marry? Would Hadrian, adopted at six, remain stubbornly Cockney, in spite of the Rockleys (and a middle-class education)? Would he contrive to emigrate to Canada at fifteen? Would Mr Rockley threaten to disinherit his daughters? Although any of these things might be possible in life, together they make us aware of Lawrence the writer, contriving the story to suit his ends. Story-tellers, of course, always contrive, but they must hide it if they are to create the illusion of life.

'**Fanny and Annie**' (first published in 1921) is a venture into comedy. Most of its jokes are simple ones, such as the misplaced aitches, the soloist's discomfiture and the minister's dismay. The story is most attractive and lifelike in showing how Fanny gradually re-adapts herself to her community after the grandeur of life as a lady's maid. The small but definite distinctions between Fanny and Harry are accurately observed. She belongs just above him in the social order of the England of 1919: one aunt has a sweetshop; another has left her two hundred pounds; she is lower-middle class, and therefore considered ladylike by Harry and his family. Lawrence uses metaphors he usually treats seriously to smile at her agonised sense of Harry's social inferiority:

> And her soul groaned, for she felt dragged down, dragged down to earth, as a bird which some dog has got down in the dust.

He is almost, but not quite, mocking his own style. Fanny does feel that Harry, although physically so attractive, is dreadfully common. He does not put on a collar to meet her train, and he carries her cases in the street. He is not even ashamed of these apparent failings. His assurance is that of 'a common man deliberately entrenched in his commonness'. The groaning of her soul contends with the 'kisses . . . in her blood', and it is here that Lawrence's comedy is most successful, on a small scale, but on a theme he took most seriously. The last twist in the conflict between class and sexuality is Harry's disgrace, which decides Fanny in his favour. The story's title is the clue. Annie Nixon is the girl whom Harry or Bill Bower or Ted Slaney 'or six or seven on 'em' may have got into trouble. It is the thought that Harry is *her* man, not Annie's, that makes up Fanny's mind, in the course of the comfortable gossiping Goodall conversation, at the close, and reconciles her to her future mother-in-law.

'**Monkey Nuts**' (first published in 1922) reverses the situation of 'You Touched Me', where a man succeeds in bullying a woman into marrying him. Miss Stokes is 'nuts' on Joe, and she 'monkeys' with him, although ultimately in vain. Lawrence has ingeniously poised Joe between the mischievous Albert, who dominates him, and the 'masterful' Miss Stokes, who wants to. He sways from hating Albert 'in his soul' to dreading and loathing her. She attracts and repels him until he is 'stupid'. He is not articulate enough to say anything about the furious undercurrents of instinct and emotion warring within him. The story's last sentence says that these are as terrifying as anything in the First World War. The tones of his voice are signs of his raw, almost animal reactions:

> 'Too many by half,' blurted out Joe, jeeringly, in a sudden fit of uncouth rudeness that made both the others stare.

'I'm not keen on going any farther,' barked out Joe, in an uncouth voice. 'She bain't my choice.'

The awkward phrasing ('not keen') shows him on the edge of control of speech: the blurts and barks of his voice say more about his feelings at the prospect of being 'mastered' by a woman than language can. Albert's talk, facile and facetious and self-dramatising, is a good contrast to Miss Stokes's wilful and Joe's confused silences.

By the standards of 1922 the story is very frank about sexual feelings. Miss Stokes's desire for Joe is at first merely appetite:

She glanced him over – save for his slender succulent tenderness she would have despised him. She sized him up in a steady look.

His reaction when she holds him in the moonlight makes good use of the telling last word.

He felt maddened, but helpless. Her arm was round his waist, she drew him closely to her with a soft pressure that made all his bones rotten.

The exchanges between Albert and Miss Stokes are also effectively blunt: '"Well, Miss Stokes, have me," he added.'

Albert's use of the phrase 'Monkey nuts' shows his irreverence for sexual relations (which is the meaning he gives the expression), a shallowness to be heard in all his chatter. Joe's use of it at the end shows that he has failed to break through his inhibitions. Miss Stokes is punished for her original aggressive use of the term; she has become vulnerable at the end, in tears, and finally white with emotion. The story pictures a remarkable triangle of sexual failure. Unrecognised sexual feelings between the men are hinted at, and no more.

The last stage of Lawrence's work in this genre, represented in two collections, *The Woman Who Rode Away* (1928) and the posthumous *The Lovely Lady* (1933), saw his interests develop in new directions. He explored combinations of modern settings with the conventions of fairy-stories and fables. He wrote social satire. He pictured the lives of richer and better-educated people. 'The Rocking-Horse Winner', 'The Man Who Loved Islands' and 'Things' are fables with characters from the English and American upper and upper-middle classes.

'The Rocking-Horse Winner' (first published in 1926) is a tall story, and a fable. Its theme is the old one of love versus money. Paul's mother is a woman who would belong to smart 1920s society if only she could afford it. To win his mother's love, Paul learns he must make her rich, and therefore he must be lucky. But the story says that love and money do not match; if magic could somehow unite them, the results would be horrible. The wooden horse is a well-chosen symbol: it is a hollow substitute for life; however furiously Paul rides, it gets him nowhere; magically, it takes him to the place 'where there is luck', but that is out of this world, and, as in fairy-stories, a place of danger. The riding is unnatural, because the boy is too old for a rocking-horse and too young to be a blade of the turf. Many phrases also imply that a dark god of sexual excitement is present in the frantic, solitary, secret rides, which he knows his mother would stop.

It is a good story about money, and about gambling, an urge too strong for many people to control, and one which entails a kind of belief in magic. Lawrence's light touch with fairy-story terms persuades the reader to suspend disbelief in Paul as the first gambler ever to have found how to be *sure*. Once we have taken that imaginative step, the fascination of winning ever-larger sums which overtakes all three members of the partnership – wiping out differences of age and class – is entirely convincing. Paul catches the excitement of talking about betting, speaking eagerly of hundreds and thousands, and of 'going down' and 'going high'. Bassett talks of bets with 'religious' solemnity. The two men's use of the boy's last horse, Malabar, while he lies dying, betting their money and his, is a good touch. Another is the increase in the house's whispering once Paul's mother has money: the impetus of gambling and spending is out of control and can only lead to Paul's fatal fall. Money, the story insists, is dangerous magic. His mother tells Paul that her family 'has been a gambling family, and you won't know till you grow up how much damage it has done'. But she has also taught him, in so many words, that money is luck, and, implicitly, that love needs money; and her loss of her son, gloating in his last words over his money and his luck, is poetic justice.

'The Man Who Loved Islands' (first published in 1927) is a fable on the theme expressed by John Donne (*c*.1572–1631), poet and preacher, in a famous phrase: 'No man is an island, entire of itself.'* A few lines later, Donne wrote: 'Any man's death diminishes me because I am involved in mankind.' Lawrence's man is not involved enough. He is an egotist who thinks he is an idealist, and the story tells of his decline, on one island after another, into misanthropy. The manner in which he tries to create an ideal society on his first island looks ominous to those who know Lawrence. He lives alone, among the workmen and their families, a detached, patriarchal figure, 'the Master'. His big collection of books and his work as a farmer represent his attempt to live 'the higher life' – a shocking thought to Lawrence. His research project is on the flowers of classical times – a dead period, and, it is implied, a dead subject. He

*Meditation XVII, *Devotions Upon Emergent Occasions*, 1624.

is only an amateur scholar, we are told, and a gentleman-farmer, and his attitude is wrong: he is trying to be a perfect man presiding in dignity over an ideal community. Life, however, will not allow it. He might have lived with Flora on the islet as a husband and father, but he resists and escapes to his northern rock because he prefers something that is abstract and impossible to the real life of a family. Humanity has disappointed him, and he turns against it, to Lawrence's amusement in the last stage of the tale. He cannot even endure the sheep. At the end the elements assail him, symbolically. He has fought against nature on his previous islands – and, the 'ghosts' imply, against human nature, turbulent and unmanageable throughout history. Worst of all, he has opposed his own human nature, choosing classical flora instead of the live Flora, and pure intellectualising instead of messy life.

'Things' (first published in 1928) is another fable which teaches that there is no higher life than life itself. The implication throughout the story is that the ineffectual Melvilles' ideals should be reinterpreted as selfishness or materialism. The opening paragraphs alternate references to 'freedom', 'beauty' or 'Indian thought' and references to the Melvilles' income of 'a little under three thousand dollars a year'. Twelve lines into the story, the question 'But what is money?' already has an ironic edge. A tone of mocking amusement is quickly established, making fun of the Melvilles' dreams of purity and perfection. To them Paris means only Impressionistic art: 'pure light . . . How lovely!' When they practise meditation, having moved on to Italy because of the war (and because the French are materialists at heart), they dream of 'a perfect world' with greed, pain and sorrow 'eliminated'. Lawrence's scorn and his amusement are nicely balanced. The real places where the Melvilles live, Paris and Florence, are equated with 'Indian thought' – conducive to high-mindedness, for a while. Idealism, we are told, needs 'something to cotton on to'. Eventually these 'poles', to which the human vines cling, all fail; even Europe turns out to be 'dead' and 'materialistic': 'they were disappointed . . . it hadn't given them quite, not *quite*, what they had expected.' Then they are left with only their souls, and their 'things'.

Lawrence's control of the comedy is so sure that the last part of the story seems inevitable, proof of the craft which went into its making. Everything is what we should expect, and also amusing. We feel sure that the Melvilles' palazzo on the Arno would be full of their 'things', the beautiful curtains, books, and *objets d'art* they would have been collecting ever since they came to Europe; that their child would be forbidden to touch and so have a dread of them; that they would in due course want to go back to America; that storing the 'things' would be a financial burden; that travelling in America seeking soul and perfection would bore them as much as Europe. Their compromise with materialist America, in which they accept a professor's salary with which to house the 'things' on campus where all can admire them, seems the inevitable ending, just what would happen, and a good satirical judgment on their flight from materialism.

The satire seems cruel because it is so accurate. Everyone has heard the voices Lawrence mimics, exclaiming at beauty and truth, 'How lovely!', or discussing France, Italy, Europe, California as 'disappointing', or worshipping the curtains. Lawrence's purpose is to make us believe that the intellectual idealising which speaks in these voices is untrue to life and can only lead to cynicism. It is facile and selfish in the Melvilles, who want the best ideas as they want the best furniture, in order to think well of themselves, and be admired. Erasmus Melville is mocked by his name, which recalls Desiderius Erasmus (1466–1536), the great Dutch scholar and humanist of the Renaissance, and the great American novelist Herman Melville (1819–91). This Erasmus, whose wife calls him Dick, is finally no longer able to deceive himself about being high-minded. Therefore, says Lawrence, he becomes a cynical academic with 'a queer, evil scholastic look of pure scepticism'. Idealism, the story asserts, leads to scepticism because both are 'pure', and both are therefore false to life.

Lawrence's short stories achieve considerable variety and range of interests. They are entertaining and often moving. They are attractive, too, in structure and style. They are most impressive in their power to combine a vivid rendering of scenes and people with a consistent and sincerely committed approach to life.

Background to composition

Much of Lawrence's fiction puts us in mind of people and places he knew. He wrote his early stories about the mining country of his childhood and youth, and he took and transformed incidents from life. An uncle, James Lawrence, was killed in a mining accident; he lived, like Walter in 'Odour of Chrysanthemums', in a cottage on a railway line, at the Brinsley crossing, near Eastwood. Lawrence may have seen his widowed Aunt Polly giving an engine-driver a cup of tea, as Elizabeth gives one to her father. Mrs Durant's annoyance when Alfred joins the Navy recalls the reaction of Lawrence's mother when his brother George enlisted in The King's Own Scottish Borderers in 1895 (when Lawrence was ten). Some later stories arose from moments which stayed vividly in his mind, others from thoughts about people he knew. 'Fanny and Annie' seems to have originated on the platform at Butterley Station, Ripley, in Derbyshire in November 1918, when Lawrence saw a man's face 'lit up red' from the foundry of the neighbouring ironworks and decided to write a story beginning with Harry Goodall meeting his ladylike girl arriving by train from Gloucestershire. In 1925 Lawrence was asked to write 'a story of the uncanny' for a collection of tales: Paul's partnership with Bassett seems to have been prompted by his having known a young girl (Leonora Brooke) who conspired with a servant to place bets on horses when her parents were away from home. 'The Rocking-Horse Winner' developed from there.*

Other stories angered friends and acquaintances by seeming to portray their lives unflatteringly, in the guise of fiction. The novelist Compton Mackenzie (1883–1972) saw 'The Man Who Loved Islands' as a libel on himself and managed to have it excluded from Secker's English edition of *The Woman Who Rode Away* (although it remained in Knopf's American edition of the same year, 1928), on the grounds that it was libellous. Mackenzie had leased Herm and Jethou, two Channel islands, in 1920, and been forced to move from Herm to Jethou, leaving behind former employees, in 1923. He had bought islands in the Outer Hebrides in October 1922. Lawrence admitted analogies in 'circumstances', but denied any intention to portray Mackenzie in the character of his islander. Mackenzie later withdrew his objection, and the story was first published in book form in England in *The Lovely Lady* (1933). Lawrence's American friends, Earl Brewster and his wife, considered that 'Things' was based on their art-collecting and interest in Buddhism. Many others in circles Lawrence frequented objected to his tactless disinclination to 'disguise', in his novels and stories, characters he had created with them in mind.

His fiction is autobiographical in many respects. We are bound to think of his parents when we read 'Odour of Chrysanthemums'. Lawrence's friend Jessie Chambers objected that his sympathy for his mother had distorted the relationship of Mr and Mrs Morel, clearly based on his parents, in *Sons and Lovers*. Elizabeth resembles Mrs Morel in her schoolteacher's English and respectable horror of 'drink', and her admission of blame can be seen as a development in Lawrence's attitude to his parents. He began the story in 1909, and was still revising it at the proof stage of *The Prussian Officer* (1914), although it was first published in 1911. It is only in the last version that Elizabeth Bates condemns herself in Lawrence's strongest terms for denying Walter in life. As he matured, Lawrence grew

*It was published in *The Ghost Book: 16 Stories of the Uncanny Compiled by Lady Cynthia Asquith*, Hutchinson, London, 1926.

increasingly hostile to the middle-class (and Nonconformist Protestant Christian) concept of 'respectability' his mother had championed, because he believed that it entailed the false values he attacked in such stories as 'The Christening' and 'Daughters of the Vicar'.

The background to the next group of stories is the First World War. Its impact was overwhelming. Lawrence feared that the 'iron rain' of war would destroy the world. War conditions intensified everything he hated in England: *Women in Love*, composed in 1916, pictures London as an inferno. Western civilisation seemed to have a 'death wish', or some disease which would kill it from within. But he also came to think that the war might be necessary for civilisation's renewal. With many of his contemporaries, he deplored Victorian England, because it had been dishonest about money, as Victorian novelists had shown, and dishonest also about the body and sexuality. He wanted the stories of *England, My England* to be honest about everything, including the most violent, unpredictable and frightening undercurrents of our nature. Only honesty about 'the whole man and woman alive', he believed, could heal civilisation. Writing 'on the side of life', he wanted to show how warlike, tempestuous and terrible even placid-looking scenes can be: a soldier walking a land-girl home, or an inspector chatting to conductresses after work. Honesty about women was a duty to the times. The fact that women had to take jobs, on trams or farms, to free men for military service, advanced female emancipation rapidly in the last years of the war. Lawrence hoped to shatter Edwardian images of shy lasses coyly smiling on chivalrous men, with the literary weapon of his violent scenes: the hysterical women tearing at John Thomas's clothes; Miss Stokes clutching Joe until his bones rot. Life could not be lived 'decently', he maintained, until truly known for the war it is.

Often accused of indecency, Lawrence had his own large and generous concept of decent life. Many of his principles were traditional, surprising only in his power to give them permanent expression in freshly written stories about the contemporary world. It is fatal to put love of money before love of your son. No man is an island. Soured idealists turn cynical. Possessions, great or small, interfere with ideals. Although he had lost his Christian faith, and although he was hostile to Christianity's concept of purity and to all absolute values, much of the background to Lawrence's stories can be found in the New Testament. He called the Bible 'a novel', meaning that as a term of the highest praise – all about, he said, 'the man alive'. Some of his contemporaries saw him, wrongly, as a prophetic figure; he may have seen himself, in some of the later satires, as a scourge of the rich and clever for their sins against life.

His own experience had taught him to mistrust ideals: he was inclined towards idealistic systems, dreaming during the war of making a new start in an American community to be founded by himself and friends, where 'decent life' might be possible. But he disliked intellectual idealising, especially in people who claimed to love 'freedom' when they meant private incomes, or claimed to be 'Buddhists' while showing off their furniture and pictures. He assumed that there must be a causal connection: purely intellectual love of values must lead to purely greedy love of things. Purity and perfection must be false goals, as both 'The Man Who Loved Islands' and 'Things' declare. Again and again, in his later polemic, he urges that there is only one true goal: we must 'live life', or be nothing. What that means, he says, we must learn in his fiction, not in any 'background' of ideas.

Structure

Lawrence designed each story to make the most of the situation, incident or idea he had chosen. He acknowledged no rules or models to be imitated. As general principles, he held that 'a perfect work of art is a lie', and that 'looseness', 'openness' and 'apparent formlessness' were better than tightly enclosed, highly organised works which aimed at perfection of form.

Among the early stories, 'Daughters of the Vicar' covers events over a long time-span, and is like a sketch for a novel, divided into parts as though into chapters: it is easy to imagine the sort of novel it might have grown into. (Lawrence used the idea of two sisters in *The Rainbow* and *Women in Love*, originally planned as 'The Sisters' at about the time the story was composed.) 'Odour of Chrysanthemums' covers only one evening, although it seems to achieve in the character of Elizabeth Bates the fullness of presentation which another writer might have hoped to accomplish in a whole novel. Comparing the story with any chapter of a novel will show how carefully its structure has been planned to make it complete and self-contained. 'Strike-Pay' seems to have grown from a miner's anecdote: 'I'll never forget the day I lost my half-sovereign.' It is told primarily for the sake of what happens; we read on to find out; once Maud forgives Ephraim there is nothing more to tell. 'The Christening' seems to have been built up to illustrate the author's ideas about will-power and 'respectability'. Its ending is 'open': we would be glad to read more.

'Tickets, Please' is partly shaped by its parallel with *The Bacchae*: the first stage establishes the strong Bacchic spirit among the corps of conductresses; the next shows how their King Pentheus outrages them – it is the scene where they all but tear him to bits which gives us the idea of the analogy with Euripides, and makes us think back to see how well it fits. 'You Touched Me' is like 'Daughters of the Vicar' in covering a long time-span, which might have been worked up into at least a novella: as it is, the story is rather overcrowded with explanations of what happened years ago, without the space to make them convincing, given such a sequence of odd events. 'Fanny and Annie' is like a playlet in several scenes, each animated, full of dialogue and bustle, with a dramatic climax in the church and a strong last line before the curtain. 'Monkey Nuts' is unusual. The familiar triangle of two men and a woman, is, if not upside-down, askew, since it is a man who is pursued. The rivals for Miss Stokes are Albert – actively, but not seriously – and Joe – passively, but in deadly earnest. In another way, Albert and Miss Stokes are rivals for Joe. The situation is so emotionally charged, and so interesting, that it would have merited treatment at greater length.

'The Rocking-Horse Winner' and 'The Man Who Loved Islands' mimic, for Lawrentian purposes, the structure and style of fairy-stories, only omitting the traditional 'Once upon a time':

There was a woman who was beautiful . . .

There was a man who loved islands.

This puts all that follows, in spite of the contemporary details, in the remote, fairy-story world where everything can be known and understood, where everything with any bearing can be quickly told, and where everything is bound to illustrate the clear moral or meaning of the tale. The magic of the first story is appropriate, and affects the structure: the story will end when the magic is worked out. We can soon see that the magic will grow until it kills Paul, and that the moral requires an ending where his mother has gained boundless wealth and lost her son. In Chaucer's words, when a tale ends, 'there is no more to say'. Where the early stories often seem brief, significant glimpses into the characters' lives, these appear to exhaust the narrative interest of the characters. We grasp the structure of 'The Man Who Loved Islands' when we see that the islands must shrink in every way, with fewer people and less purpose on each. The Master tries to fill the first island with his ego; the last island diminishes him to next to nothing. He has offended the powers of nature and they have imprisoned him in their elements. The story is not quite an allegory, but it has something of an allegory's steady, inevitable progress to a foreseeable end. 'Things' is also shaped like a fable. The Melvilles' journey of escape from materialism takes them all the way back again because, we are meant to see, they never really start. They collect 'things' from the first day. The structure is ironic, an interweaving of 'things' and ideals.

They looked upon their home as a place entirely furnished by loveliness, not by 'things' at all.

This is a neat preparation for the burden the things will become, eventually costing so much to store that the idealists have to go to Ohio to settle down.

Various patterns, ironic, symbolic and verbal, structure the stories. Elizabeth Bates tells her children, thinking that Walter will be dead drunk tonight, 'I won't wash him', and 'He can lie on the floor'; these are words for us to remember when she and Walter's mother lay out and wash his body. Such ironies join different scenes and stages of the narrative, making us think back and read again. Each time the chrysanthemums are mentioned, we sense another pattern, woven into the events and giving them meaning, turning their odour from one of life to one of death. The rocking-horse, standing in 'an arrested prance in the boy's bedroom', contrasts well with the race-horses he 'knows', careering to their victories; the stillness of the image also has an ominous hint of his fall. Verbal patterns shape some stories in particular. The phrase 'Monkey nuts' begins and ends Joe's relations with Miss Stokes: she insults Joe with it and he flings it back. Albert makes a joke of it, until, imposing his cold authority, he says, 'Work's work, and nuts is nuts.' The patterning of the stories by key words connects structure with style.

Style

Lawrence is at his best in descriptions. The first paragraph of 'Odour of Chrysanthemums' blends country and colliery, as in all his Nottinghamshire landscapes. Verbs of motion animate the passage. The colt in the gorse 'out-distances' the coal train; birds 'pull' at scarlet hips by the track; the engine's smoke 'sinks' and 'cleaves' to the rough grass; flames 'lick' at the ashy sides of the pit-bank; the black trucks 'clank', 'stumble', 'thump' and 'jolt', heavy and ugly, while the leaves 'drop noiselessly'; dusk 'creeps' into the spinney; the wheels of the headstocks 'spin' against the sky. 'The Man Who Loved Islands' is full of good impressions of islands; Lawrence was, in a different sense, another such man as the 'hero' of the story.

> He walked over the wet, springy turf, and dark-grey sheep tossed away from him, spectral, bleating hoarsely. And he came to the dark pool, with the sedge. Then on in the dampness, to the grey sea sucking angrily among the rocks.
> This was indeed an island.

Here again, words which evoke movement give the writing life: the islander walks in 'springy' turf and 'on in the dampness', while the sheep 'toss away' and the sea 'sucks'. Lawrence had an extraordinary awareness of animals and could put this into words. The pit-ponies out of the pit in 'Strike-Pay' are 'dazed', 'dreary', 'inert', 'blank', while the sap swells all around them on a beautiful 'growing day': the pit has unhorsed them. There is a remarkable gull on the islander's last island:

> And as the gull walked back and forth, back and forth in front of the cabin, strutting on pale-dusky gold feet, holding up his pale yellow beak that was curved at the tip, with curious alien importance, the man wondered over him. He was portentous, he had a meaning.

Lawrence could also put his feeling for houses into his writing.

> Mr Lindley passed round the low wall, and descended the low steps that led from the highway down to the cottage which crouched darkly and quietly away below the rumble of passing trains and the clank of coal-carts, in a quiet little underworld of its own.

This house in 'Daughters of the Vicar', probably described from memory of a cottage near the railway at Brinsley, is, rightly, more human than the bird: it crouches, sheltering from the alien trains. Lawrence also conveys in the same story how human gardens and trees can become.

> Then the bunches of snow in the twigs of the apple tree that leaned towards the fence told her she must go and see Mrs Durant. The tree was in Mrs Durant's garden.

Snow is vividly described in 'Daughters of the Vicar', Lawrence seeing it both as an alien element, and as a part of the human world, printed, besmirched, trampled to slush. Here it 'tells' Louisa where to go when she notices the 'bunches' the twigs are strong enough to hold. Lawrence's descriptions are often poetic, combining precise observation with figurative language. In 'Strike-Pay' the white and purple crocuses 'blaze' in Nuttall churchyard in 'tiny tongues of flame'. Mrs Bates's chrysanthemums are 'dishevelled . . . like pink cloths hung on bushes'. Lawrence often prefers, as in these stories, to indicate a season by means of its flowers, rather than name it.

He has many uses for figurative language. Metaphor conveys emotion. In 'The Christening' Bertha's momentary delight in the baby, when she is not treating its mother 'like dirt', is a 'streak of light to her'. Repulsion is often conveyed in metaphor or simile. Mr Rowbotham's daughters 'shrink' when they hear his voice raised in joy. The conductresses avoid John Thomas, after their assault, 'as if he had been an electric wire'. The idealists' child Peter in 'Things' avoids the things, in the Florence house, 'as if they had been nests of sleeping cobras' or the Ark of the Covenant. People become animals. Joe in 'Monkey Nuts' is a dog. At first he has 'some of the look of a dog which is going to bite', when he eyes Miss Stokes; later, when mastered by Albert, he stands 'with his tail between his legs'. Hadrian is like the rat in 'You Touched Me'. He has the courage of a cornered rat, and also 'some of the neatness, the reserve, the underground quality of the rat' – the term is not at all derogatory in this story (although it is so in 'Things'). The islander is 'a queer, caged animal' in the eyes of his bailiff, who sees what he will have become by the time of the third island. Characters are not confined to one animal comparison. Apart from his doglike aspect, Joe is 'a very shy bird'.

There is more figurative and poetic writing in some stories than in others. 'The Man Who Loved Islands' stands out in this respect. The spirit of the first island is 'resentful':

> You could feel, down in the wet, sombre hollows, the resentful spirit coiled upon itself, like a wet dog coiled in gloom, or a snake that is neither asleep nor awake.

The island is also a universe, full of the souls of the dead; it annihilates the solid earth; 'and your slippery, naked dark soul finds herself out in the timeless world'. Men of Gaul, Anglo-Saxon missionaries and Vikings return in the nights, from the Channel Islands' past, to make 'our' islander 'uneasy'. 'Odour of Chrysanthemums' has a more muted but perhaps more powerful poetic quality, in its symbol, in the image of Elizabeth's dismayed 'soul' standing apart from her, and in the way the archetypal scene of mother and wife tending the naked corpse is rendered particular by details which picture the cottage where Walter lies in his pit-dirt. The mother's 'big black bonnet', too big when she and Elizabeth kneel on each side of the body so that it brushes the widow's hair, is a good detail, visual and tactile.

Lawrence's imagery succeeds wherever his exact observation is at work. Sometimes he is vague, conventional and reiterative: blood burns and freezes, bodies are stone or water; marrying Mr Massy, in 'Daughters of the Vicar', Mary is 'a pure reason', 'a pure will', 'purely just', 'a pure will', in the space of eight lines. Lawrence has a motive, in attacking the word 'pure'; he is urging that purity is unhealthy; but passages of this kind are those most likely, in the novels as well as the short stories, to be skipped by some readers.

The stories make relatively little use of allusion. 'The Man Who Loved Islands' refers to Hermes and the Hesperides, but that is appropriate because the islander is a classicist. 'Tickets, Please' expects only a vague recollection of *The Bacchae*, one of the best-known works of ancient literature; and Thermopylae, Annie's tram-platform, is not an obscure allusion. Lawrence's imagination does, however, often draw on the Bible. In 'Fanny and Annie' Harry in the choir is Baalam's ass, and if the analogy seems blurred, that suits Fanny's bad memory of her Sunday-schooling. In 'You Touched Me' Matilda is Mary to Emmie's Martha, a conventional contrast which the girls must have heard many times, and probably accepted. The islander is said to be unlike Abraham because he has no ambition for his offspring to be as numberless as the sands of the sea-shore – a remark he himself might have made. His farm-hand's wife thinks that the first island is one of the lean kine of Egypt, because it swallows so much money. She, like the other 'people', is not an islander and means to say so. Lawrence also likes to allude to fairy-stories and nursery rhymes.

The narrative styles are varied. The prose often resembles the style of an informal speaker talking about the events, although there is more feeling and imagination than is commonly heard in talk in England today.

> There was no mistake about it, Annie liked John Thomas a good deal. She felt so rich and warm in herself whenever he was near. And John Thomas really liked Annie, more than usual. The soft, melting way in which she could flow into a fellow, as if she melted into his very bones, was something rare and good. He fully appreciated this.

The lyrical notes – 'flow into a fellow' – merge well with the conversational style – 'no mistake about it'. There is a change in the next sentences:

> But with a developing acquaintance there began a developing intimacy. Annie wanted to consider him a person, a man: she wanted to take an intelligent interest in him, and to have an intelligent response.

The balanced phrases, the diction, and the use of the colon to develop the second sentence are more formal and analytical. Sometimes the narrative seems to mimic Annie's speech-habits.

> After all, he had a wonderfully warm, cosy way of holding a girl . . . And, after all, it was pleasant . . . And, after all, he was so warm . . .

Lawrence's art yields Annie to John Thomas in these 'after all's'; but the phrase is hers. Elsewhere the writing is sharply removed from her

point of view. She would not make a joke about Thermopylae.
Lawrence can be effective with short sentences. In this story (two
paragraphs after 'There was no mistake about it'), we find, in the
space of seven lines:

Here she made a mistake.

He hated intelligent interest.

So he left her.

Sentences beginning 'And . . .' often sound colloquial. Sometimes
they echo the style of the Authorised Version of the Bible (1611).
This is most noticeable towards the end of 'Odour of Chrysanthemums':

And he was the father of her children . . . She looked at his face,
and she turned her own face to the wall. For his look was other
than hers, his way was not her way. She had denied him what he
was – she saw it now.

The plain diction and strong cadences echo passages in the
Authorised Version, here and throughout this section of the story.
Antithetical sentences – 'his look . . . his way' – sound biblical. The
intrusive 'him' in 'She had denied him' recalls the seventeenth-
century structure, 'I know you what you are'. The effect is
appropriate for this moment of revelation, religious in force and
consequence for Lawrence and for his character. Elizabeth might
speak to herself in words and rhythm such as these.

There are other styles in later stories, where parody and mimicry
become elements of Lawrence's art. 'The Rocking-Horse Winner'
mimics the language and style of fairy-stories, lightly mocking their
simplicity: 'She married for love, and the love turned to dust.' The
technique is reminiscent of Charles Dickens (1812–70). The
children's toys hear the 'whispering' about 'more money':

It came whispering from the springs of the still-swaying rocking-
horse, and even the horse, bending his wooden champing head,
heard it. The big doll, sitting so pink and smirking in her new pram,
could hear it quite plainly, and seemed to be smirking all the more
self-consciously because of it.

The writing sounds childish but the knowledge of the power of money
is mature, in this and other such playful passages, in Lawrence as in
Dickens. The voice is amused, detached and ironic. We hear it again
in 'The Man Who Loved Islands': 'At this very moment, it happened
there was an auction of islands.' It amuses this narrator to talk of
islands as pieces of property to be bought and taken home. Lawrence
is obliquely mocking the islander's possessive attitude, emphasising

the point that the islands never really are his. The narrative of 'Things' mimics the voices of its characters. Italics often signal the emphasis we are to imagine in the speech of the idealists: 'although they still *loved* "Indian thought"'; 'Greed, pain, and sorrow must either be eliminated from *all the world*, or else, what was the use . . .'. The result often is that the story says the opposite: they do not love Indian thought; the Melvilles do not really care about all the world.

Dialogue is another aspect of style in fiction. It could be said that the dialect of Nottinghamshire was one of Lawrence's two native languages. Such a 'bilingualism' is a great strength in his novels and stories. Many English novelists have used dialect only for comedy, as though it were inherently ridiculous (a tendency in English literature since the sixteenth century). Lawrence finds dialect amusing in 'Fanny and Annie'. Elsewhere, it is dignified, as in 'Odour of Chrysanthemums'.

> 'I don't like leaving the children in bed, and nobody in the house,' she said.
> 'No, you dunna!' he replied courteously.

In exchanges such as Elizabeth Bates's with the Rigleys, standard English tends to sound cold and distant. Dialect in Lawrence is warm and caressing. Its speakers share the comfort of a community, and Elizabeth seems excluded here from the sympathy she might have received. 'Strike-Pay' shows that dialect can be a comfort and a defence. The gang assert themselves when the Colonel has passed, with exclamations in broader dialect than they have been using, calling out 'Sorry' (that is, 'mate' or 'pal'). When Ephraim's mother-in-law attacks him in speech which she thinks 'polite', he takes refuge in dialect. In his broad Derbyshire, he feels a man. In other stories, dialect is an offensive weapon, as it is in 'Daughters of the Vicar' when the miners' wives call out to the vicar that they are 'throng' (busy). Mrs Goodall in 'Fanny and Annie' puts up her very broad dialect as a defensive and offensive weapon against Fanny's 'ladylike' speech, although secretly admiring her. Such superior English, she feels, should not go unrebuked in her house. Dialect speech in the stories is artificial: in life it would be less deft, more obscure – and more obscene – than Lawrence makes his characters' speech, but all literary dialogue is unrealistic in ways of this kind. It must seem lifelike, but it must also be clearer and more entertaining than most people really are.

Lawrence is equally good at dialogue in standard English, in Paul's preparatory-school colloquialisms ('Honour bright!'), in the idealists' affectations ('Lovely!' – a word Lawrence hated to hear insincerely said), in the prim Mr Lindley ('There is no *dishonour*, surely, in serving in the Navy?'), and in people such as Fanny whose English is not quite correct ('Harry . . . wouldn't think the Queen was any too good for him, if he's a mind to her'). He is good, too, with biblical speakers, influenced by the language of the Authorised Version. The minister in 'The Christening' speaks a relatively pure form of it ('A man child is born unto us'), while Mr Rowbotham chats familiarly with God in his prayer, mixing the cadences of his dialect with those learned at the chapel.

Characters

Much has already been said about characters in these Notes: all elements in fiction tend to be inter-related, and especially so in the confined space of a short story. Every phrase and image counts for more in a short story than in a novel, where so much more evidence is offered and we live with the characters over a long period of reading. Conception, structure, narrative style, images and dialogue all contribute to building the characters. At the end of 'Things', Erasmus is compared to a rat in a cage. He comments on the satisfactions of materialistic America in a phrase which catches the tone of his comfortable, middle-aged cynicism: 'Europe's the mayonnaise all right, but America supplies the good old lobster – what?' This image and this tone of voice are the culmination of the satirical contempt which has been developing throughout the narrative. Even more than is the case in a novel, short-story characters have to be considered in relation to one another: even the lonely islander is vividly seen through the eyes of his bailiff; Elizabeth Bates, in 'Odour of Chrysanthemums', is inseparable from her relations, neighbours and husband; in 'Monkey Nuts' we cannot think of Joe apart from Albert and Miss Stokes; in 'Things' the fact that his wife merely sheds her ideals emphasises the corruption of Erasmus's, turned to an 'evil' scepticism.

Some characters are interesting in themselves; others exist for the sake of the stories. In 'Strike-Pay' Ephraim behaves and reacts in the ways we would expect of any young miner, showing off on the pony, ashamed when his mates share their pay with him, afraid of his mother-in-law: he is not interesting in himself. Others fit into conventional roles: Matilda and Emmie, in 'You Touched Me', are Mary and Martha. The characters are quite ordinary in 'The Rocking-Horse Winner': the mother too greedy for 'luxury', Paul a bright boy wanting mother-love, Oscar an amiable uncle, and Bassett a seemly servant. What happens is extraordinary. Lawrence sums up the Annie of 'Tickets, Please' in a sentence: 'She was a plump, quick, alive little creature'. These are terms of praise, and all that matters. Annie is not meant to be very different from the other young women on the trams, less vindictive than Nora Purdy, we are told, but a typical bold, sensitive, good-natured girl, which is what the story needs. How she reacts when she feels insulted and then when she is 'chosen' is what matters; we are to think her feelings typical of any decent girl, and approve the emancipation of the world of the trams. Characters are the main interest in other stories. 'Monkey Nuts' keeps us wondering about those of its triangle. The two sisters and their men in 'Daughters of the Vicar' are observed and discussed as individuals. The islands, their past history, their weather, their animals and their people all exist for the sake of the man who loved islands. These people are all conceived, however, in relation to Lawrence's ideas about life.

There is a difference between what a story tells and what it renders, in the sense of showing an action, letting us hear a voice or form an image of a character for ourselves. We are told that the idealists of 'Things' 'wisely' did not 'build their lives' on their son Peter, and we hear the measured note of irony in 'wisely'. When we are shown the child nervously skirting around the 'things', afraid to touch, as though avoiding 'a nest of sleeping cobras', we see into his parents, whom these lines show to be, in Lawrence's terms, 'false to life'. Lawrence had a genius for rendering characters, sometimes in an image or a phrase. We 'see' Alfred (Louisa's word for discovering the whole man alive) when he 'mechanically' hands her back the soap. It is a good moment in 'Monkey Nuts' when Albert, commenting on his being 'the one extra', addresses his words to the moon. He then bows and salutes before he leaves. In 'Fanny and Annie', Fanny enjoys the dramatic touch of her last line. We might wonder if it is the opportunity of staging her decision in this way which makes up her mind. Lawrence is like Dickens in his ability to show how people such as Albert and Fanny dramatise themselves.

Lawrence also tells us about his characters. He tells us in 'The Christening' that Mr Rowbotham's children are 'brutal' and 'self-willed' and 'only half-individuals'. When he tells us that the minister 'had never mixed with life, and women were all unliving, Biblical things to him', the touch of wit in the last phrase saves the sentence, but in the first clause Lawrence seems to be merely abusing his character. There is more telling than rendering in 'The Christening', although what is shown is good. What he tells us about Alfred's failure to break through his inhibitions to achieve a satisfying sexual relationship in 'Daughters of the Vicar' is shown more effectively in the plight of Joe in 'Monkey Nuts'. Some readers feel that Lawrence tells too much and is sometimes needlessly reiterative in the telling.

He would have said that this is a characteristic of his work, not a fault. He did not want to write perfect works of art; looseness, roughness, and even violence in the narrative, were sometimes part of his method. It is true that we can hear, in passages where he seems to raise his voice to denounce a character, his excitement and commitment to the world he was creating.

The short story suited his talent in several respects. He was chiefly interested in people's most difficult and intense emotional experiences. One critic has rightly remarked of characters in his novels that 'persons habitually living at such a pitch could not long avoid nervous disintegration'.* It can be seen, even in the masterpieces, *The Rainbow* and *Women in Love*, that he sometimes misrepresents human life in ignoring its flatness and always seeking its intensities. Short stories, depicting at most a few scenes, can concentrate on the crises of their characters' lives, and many of Lawrence's are of this kind. The close and conspicuous interrelationships of all parts of a short story also suit his gift for connecting landscapes, climates and other aspects of setting with his portrayal of character. The coming of dusk in the first paragraph of 'Odour of Chrysanthemums', and the darkness of the room, before the children insist on the lamp being lit, is connected with the darkness in Elizabeth. The ghosts in 'The Man Who Loved Islands' are in the island because they are in the man. The racing, lurching, dangerous trams of 'Tickets, Please' have put fighting spirit into the conductresses. Alfred Durant finds the underground world of the mine easy and enjoyable because it is exclusively male: he must ascend, however, into the world of women, as he must, rising into fuller consciousness, in his own nature. The short story restricts a writer to one or two aspects of a character and this suits Lawrence's preoccupation with his characters as wives, husbands, fathers, daughters, sons and lovers. He often refers to them by role rather than by name: 'the mother', 'the husband'. 'The Rocking-Horse Winner' always refers to 'Paul's mother' or 'the mother', emphasising that it is in this failed role that we are to think of her.

Lawrence's aim was 'the whole man and woman alive', and personality in his fiction is inseparable from the physical characteristics. Success or failure in living makes people radiant or ugly. The minister in 'The Christening' is a failure in life: 'He, big and ugly, shone with a kind of unreal love.' The old miner's muscular disease emphasises the force and will of his mind. Lawrence constantly draws attention to parts of the body. In 'You Touched Me', Hadrian's bare neck is the most telling thing about him. A gentleman would always wear a collar (as Fanny knows) in the presence of

*J. I. M. Stewart, *Eight Modern Writers*, Clarendon Press, Oxford, 1963, p. 517.

women. Hadrian's neglect shows his plebeian aggression, social and sexual. In the end Matilda submits to the sight of it, as well as to the 'touch'. Hadrian sees her 'quality' in her tapering fingers. In 'Daughters of the Vicar', Alfred's face looking out at Louisa through the black soot which obscures it is not only well described: it fits the idea of her effort to 'see' him as she has never seen anyone except her sister. Cynicism dehumanises Erasmus's face in 'Things', putting a rat's look into his eyes and nose so that it is a surprise, the story says, that he does not sprout rat's whiskers. The characters are acutely conscious of one another's faces and expressions, bodies and stances, and of their 'presence'. The bailiff sees something unmanly in the 'versatility' of the Master's lips in 'The Man Who Loved Islands'. Louisa loves Alfred's peculiar ears. Mr Massy looks 'queer and obliterated' in the presence of the sun-burned Alfred.

Social class is always related to character. His class is ineradicably engrained in Hadrian by the age of six, Lawrence asserts, and his manners are therefore uncouthly plebeian (although miners are usually courteous). Louisa's struggle to 'see' Alfred is impeded by her sense that he is alien in being a working man, but she also resents his using his 'inferiority' as a weapon against her. Fanny groans in her soul when she thinks how common Harry is, but she too battles through 'the social barrier' (a common phrase in Lawrence), and so, it appears, does Matilda. The miner's children are awed, but hatred stirs in their hearts because they feel 'inferior in themselves' when they see the vicar's children filing into church in 'Daughters of the Vicar'. The gang of miners in 'Strike-Pay' is daunted by the Colonel. The clash between social and sexual instincts is at the centre of Lawrence's interest in people; he was aware from experience of the strength of social barriers in England.

Lawrence was sure that people differ radically in being male or female (not an assumption shared by all novelists). The male in Massy is strong in spite of his bodily weakness, but it is raw and unpleasant. Mary senses it when she accepts him.

> She could see him making some movement towards her, could feel the male in him, something cold and triumphant, asserting itself.

Joe senses the female in Miss Stokes as something predatory, and he shrinks away. Mothering, which Lawrence thinks essential in the female, can enrich a man's quality. Harry appeals to Fanny because 'there was something of a mother's lad about him – something warm and playful and really sensitive'. All the possessive instincts of women, including mothering, are, however, powerful and dangerous forces in the stories; and many of the characters have to contend with them.

Part 4

Hints for study

Study topics

These topics are related to the earlier parts of these Notes.

Introduction

(1) How did Lawrence's parents influence his early life?
(2) Lawrence grew up in a mining village; how did this affect his attitude to English society?
(3) Why did Lawrence want to leave England?
(4) What did Lawrence think of the effects of industrial development in England in the nineteenth century?
(5) Which writers influenced Lawrence, and how? What shortcomings did he see in earlier novelists?

Summaries

(1) List characters under these headings: mothers, fathers, sons, daughters, husbands, wives, lovers. What comparisons and contrasts can you find?
(2) Which of the stories are divided into numbered sections? Can you see any reason for the divisions? Comment on the endings and openings of sections.
(3) List turning-points in the stories. For example, 'Strike-Pay' turns on the pony-riding and loss of the half-sovereign. There may be more than one turning-point.
(4) Consider the extent and passage of time in each story. How are past events narrated? For example, how do we learn about Walter's earlier life in 'Odour of Chrysanthemums' or Hadrian's in 'You Touched Me'?
(5) In 'Odour of Chrysanthemums', what are Elizabeth's dealings with the other characters?
(6) How does her attitude to Walter change?
(7) Trace the course of Ephraim's day in 'Strike-Pay'.
(8) In 'The Christening', what is the role of each of Mr Rowbotham's children?
(9) What is his attitude to his children?
(10) In 'Daughters of the Vicar', how are the stories of the two

couples contrasted? How does the narrative alternate and interconnect them?

(11) In 'Tickets, Please', explain the role of John Thomas.

(12) In 'You Touched Me', how is the moment of the touch prepared for? What are we told about Matilda, and about Hadrian? How does Matilda come to accept Hadrian?

(13) In 'Fanny and Annie', how does Fanny make up her mind?

(14) In 'Monkey Nuts', trace the course of Joe's relations with Miss Stokes. How does Albert influence them?

(15) In 'The Rocking-Horse Winner', what are the stages in Paul's rise to wealth?

(16) What are the gradual stages in his downfall?

(17) In 'The Man Who Loved Islands', what happens on each island?

(18) In 'Things', what are the idealists' ideals?

(19) What is the role of the 'things'?

(20) Make maps of the stories: one to show Nottingham and the surrounding country; one to show the British Isles; and one to show the travels of the idealists in 'Things'.

Commentary

Nature, purpose and achievement

(1) What did Lawrence mean by 'truth to life'?

(2) What are the three stages in his story-writing?

(3) How does symbolism contribute to the stories?

(4) What do the stories say about money?

(5) What do they say about 'respectability'?

(6) How do social differences interfere with courtship and marriage?

(7) How do parents influence children in the stories?

(8) How does Lawrence present a 'war of the sexes'?

(9) How does he use analogies with Euripides's *The Bacchae* in 'Tickets, Please'?

(10) Is 'You Touched Me' entirely convincing?

(11) What kind of comedy is 'Fanny and Annie'?

(12) How are the last three stories different from the earlier work?

(13) How does Lawrence use fairy-story conventions?

Background to composition

(1) How did Lawrence draw on his impressions of friends and acquaintances?

(2) How did his relationship with his mother influence his fiction?

(3) How did the First World War influence his mind?

(4) What did he mean by 'honesty' in fiction?
(5) What did he regard as 'sins against life'?
(6) What did he think about idealism?

Structure
(1) Had Lawrence any general principles of structure?
(2) How do the stories differ in structure?
(3) What patterns can be seen in the stories?
(4) Does a second reading of a story reveal new aspects of its structure?
(5) Are some stories more 'loose' than others?
(6) Which stories depend for their structure on contrasts?
(7) How does irony contribute to structure?
(8) How does symbolism contribute?

Style
(1) Illustrate Lawrence's descriptive powers.
(2) How does he use verbs in descriptions?
(3) How does he describe houses?
(4) How does he use figurative language?
(5) Which stories include 'poetic' writing? What is 'poetic' writing in prose?
(6) What sort of allusions are there in the stories?
(7) What varieties of narrative style can be distinguished?
(8) Comment on the sentences beginning 'And . . .'.
(9) What styles do the later stories mimic?
(10) Comment on the use of dialogue.

Background

Read more stories. 'The White Stocking', 'The Prussian Officer' and 'The Horse-Dealer's Daughter' are rightly famous.

Lawrence worked at and reworked 'The White Stocking' over many years, before it was published in *The Prussian Officer* in 1914. He began with an anecdote of his mother's and ended with a story of a girl's love for one man and sexual desire for another. Ted and Elsie Whiston have been married for two years. He is a salesman; she used to work at Sam Adams's lace factory. On 14 February, Elsie receives valentines; one is in the form of a white stocking with pearl ear-rings in the toe. She admits to Whiston she received a stocking last year: now she has a pair. She does not tell him about the pearls. She tells him she thinks the stocking is from Sam Adams. Whiston is angry and jealous, but Elsie is 'stimulated all the day'. She loves her husband, but he is 'the permanent basis from which she took these giddy little flights into nowhere' – enjoying the ear-rings and dreaming about Sam Adams.

Two years ago she and Whiston went to the Christmas party given by Sam, a bachelor of forty with a reputation as a womaniser. He and Elsie danced, to Whiston's anger. Although in love with Ted, Elsie adored dancing with Adams: he had such a way of talking, which made an 'intimate animal call to her', and his touch in the 'delicious embrace' of the dance carried her helplessly away, 'unwilling, yet delighted'. She seemed to 'swim into him' in 'fusion': she felt she would 'fuse down into perfect unconsciousness at his feet and knees'. Whiston 'sat feeling heavy and dulled with rage'. Reaching for her handkerchief during the dancing, she found she had brought a white stocking instead, and dropped it in surprise. Adams pocketed it. Whiston, 'black with rage' about this incident, was restrained from violence only by 'something . . . pitiful' about her mouth. 'Be good to me', she pleaded; amazed, and 'white hot with love', Whiston took her home.

After that she stopped working at Adams's and, since their marriage, her husband has always been 'the ground of her happiness'. Nonetheless, Whiston is dull, and she has become 'used to him, as to the air she breathed'. When last year's stocking came, containing a brooch, she kept quiet about it. Now she plans that her mother will 'give' her the ear-rings. What fun if Adams saw her wearing them! Whiston comes home in a bad temper; 'the male in him' has been 'uneasy' all day. Has she burned the stocking? She puts on both stockings and raises her skirt to show her legs; then dances about the room. They quarrel; he insults her; she tells him about the other gifts; he strikes her, filled with 'lust to see her bleed'. She weeps with rage; she will not be 'bullied'. He sends the presents back to Adams. At the close he cries 'My love, my little love' in 'anguish of spirit', since her tear-stained face is so pathetic.

This story may be compared with 'Tickets, Please' in the ways the physical contact of the lovers is imagined and described, and in the violence, stirred by insult and betrayal, followed by distress – emotions not understood in either story by those who experience them.

Violence also erupts from subconscious depths in the two characters of the title story of *The Prussian Officer*. The Captain is a haughty Prussian aristocrat; unmarried at forty, he takes a mistress from time to time, but has never had a true relationship with a woman. He has 'the look of a man who fights with life'. His eyes are 'always flashing with cold fire'. The Captain's orderly, a conscript of twenty-two, has 'dark, expressionless eyes that make him seem never to have thought, only to have received life direct through his senses, and acted straight from instinct'. The presence of his servant begins to infuriate the Captain.

He could not get away from the sense of the youth's person, while he was in attendance. It was like a warm flame upon the older man's tense, rigid body, that had become almost unliving, fixed. There was something so free and self-contained about him, and something in the young fellow's movement, that made the officer aware of him. And this irritated the Prussian. He did not choose to be touched into life by his servant.

The story gradually develops this contrast between the two men. The officer is all will-power, intellect and discipline, in the head; the servant is all sensuousness, instinct, 'unconscious' openness to life, in the body. The conflict between them is inevitable. The Captain's fighting against life has corrupted him, and he derives 'a thrill of deep pleasure', although also a feeling of shame, from beating and kicking the young man, and otherwise tormenting him – keeping him at work when he might be with his girl. One evening the servant is savagely kicked and bullied because he has been writing verses for the girl. Afterwards the officer stands motionless for an hour, 'a chaos of sensations'; then he denies to himself that anything has happened.

The servant is bewildered, mesmerised by the cold, blue eyes, and helpless before the Captain's will, reluctant, above all, to be forced out of his unthinking life and 'into consciousness'. He has to pretend that the other man does not exist, 'so that he himself might live'. After a long, painful march, the psychological pressure becomes unbearable and he kills the Captain. The orderly's desertion, and death by exhaustion and exposure occupy the rest of the story. A night storm, the sight of distant mountains and the deadly 'drilling' of the sun next day reflect the inner 'darkness' of the youth's failure to mature into a 'conscious' man who might have faced out the Captain. A reading of 'The Prussian Officer' shows better than any definition Lawrence's conception of 'the whole man alive'; it helps in various ways with our reading of other stories. The orderly is like Alfred Durant in his easy, unthinking existence, and like Joe in 'Monkey Nuts', in revulsion from a stronger will. The horrible result of the Captain's lifetime of casual affairs with women helps us to appreciate what is wrong in John Thomas Raynor in 'Tickets, Please'. The symbolic landscape at the end might be compared with that of the last section of 'The Man Who Loved Islands'.

Although 'The Horse-Dealer's Daughter' was first published in 1922, it was started in 1916, at the time of Lawrence's worst misgivings about the war and the 'death wish' of Western man. It is a story of attempted suicide, by the daughter, Mabel, and her 'resurrection', achieved by a man who rescues her and immediately, almost against his will, becomes her lover. The story opens with the plight of the horse-dealer's grown-up children now that he has died and left only debts that cannot be paid. The three brothers are going to accept lives of 'subjection'. They suggest, mockingly, that Mabel might find work as a servant. Since the time of her mother's death, when Mabel was fourteen, the girl has lived on memories of her. Now she puts flowers on the grave, and goes to find 'the world of death she had inherited'. Jack Ferguson, a poor young country doctor, sees her walking into a pond and goes after her. Reviving her on the bank, undressing her and wrapping her in blankets by the fire at home, he thinks of himself only as a doctor, saving life. When life fully returns to Mabel, she greets him as her lover, and his will yields, 'horribly' and 'wonderfully'. The 'horrid stagnant smell' of the pond, symbolising death, is, by the end of the story, behind them, although it lingers in her hair. Tomorrow, Ferguson says in the last lines, he means to marry her. Lawrence's first title for this story was 'The Miracle'. He uses biblical images and language, with connotations of the Resurrection, but this is a miracle in Lawrence's personal religion of life and love. The biblical language might be compared with that of 'Odour of Chrysanthemums', but the effect of the story is the opposite: life can sometimes be kind. Even the First World War, Lawrence thought, might result in renewal, if people would give themselves wholly to life.

Other stories which connect war and sexuality include 'England, My England' and 'The Mortal Coil'. Also from Lawrence's second collection of stories, 'Samson and Delilah' is another example of how his imagination drew on the Bible. From among the later stories, 'Jimmy and the Desperate Woman' might be read together with 'Things'; Jimmy lives in books rather than in life: his 'literary' ideal of a woman is ironically mocked. Story-readers who want to advance to reading the novels should begin with Sons and Lovers, which has many obvious links with the early stories, especially in Paul's possessive love, and in Mrs Morel's war – like that of Elizabeth Bates, although viewed differently – against her husband. The Rainbow and Women in Love, Lawrence's most ambitious books, are more difficult, and more rewarding. (York Notes are available on all three novels.) Many of Lawrence's poems are immediately enjoyable and impressive, although they merit many re-readings. Begin with 'Snake' and 'The Mosquito'; then try 'Bavarian Gentians' and 'The Ship of Death'. 'Innocent England' is an entertaining poem, written after Lawrence's paintings had been seized by the police in 1929. He pretends that he had not known his pictures would be unacceptable in England if they lacked fig-leaves:

Virginal, pure policemen came
and hid their faces for very shame,

while they carried the shameful things away
to gaol, to be hid from the light of day.

Lawrence usually attacks or ridicules the term 'pure'. Here, his touch is light, and very convincing.

Another kind of background reading involves exploring the genre of the short story. Katherine Mansfield's 'The Garden Party' appears in many anthologies and in the reprint by Penguin Books (Harmondsworth, 1951, often reprinted) of her collection *The Garden Party* (1922). It might interestingly be compared and contrasted with Lawrence's work: it is effectively symbolic; by his standards, too perfect and pure. James Joyce's *Dubliners*, available in paperback, was published in 1914, the same year as *England, My England*. In 'Eveline', a girl fails to find the courage to board the ship on which she is to run away to get married, because she has never learned to make decisions for herself. The story is clear, strong, and offers, in its symbolism and figurative writing, scope for comparison and contrast with Lawrence. He would probably have told us explicitly, as Joyce does not, what the story implies about the effects of her upbringing. One attraction of the genre of the short story is that it is so easy to explore quickly; students of Lawrence's stories should read as widely as possible, bearing Lawrence in mind and reflecting on how he would have treated a given situation, character, incident, or theme.

The two volumes of Lawrence's assorted prose works, *Phoenix* I and II, although formidable to read through, are good for browsing. Among his essays, 'Why the Novel Matters' contains many famous pronouncements and sets out clearly his creed of 'the whole man and woman alive'. It begins:

We have a curious idea of ourselves. We think of ourselves as a body with a spirit in it, or a body with a soul in it, or a body with a mind in it . . .
It is a funny sort of superstition.

Lawrence goes on to describe his hand, writing on the page 'so cleverly', and to deny that there is any 'huge difference' between the hand and the mind which guides it. The hand explores a 'strange universe in touch' and knows 'a vast number of things'. Lawrence is as much in his hand as in his mind: there is 'me which is more me than my hand is'. He then becomes combative. A novelist knows this truth; 'a parson, or a philosopher, or a scientist, or a stupid person' does not: 'these damned philosophers, they talk as if they suddenly went off in steam, and were then much more important than they are when they're in their shirts.' Religion, philosophy and science are alike in failing to grasp 'that nothing is important but life'. Religion values soul; philosophy values mind; science values matter. Lawrence states his position:

> Now I absolutely flatly deny that I am a soul, or a body, or a mind, or an intelligence, or a brain, or a nervous system, or a bunch of glands, or any of the rest of these bits of me . . . I am man alive, and as long as I can, I intend to go on being man alive.
> For this reason I am a novelist.

As a novelist, he claims to be superior to saint, scientist, philosopher and even poet, because only the novelist goes 'the whole hog'.

> The novel is the one bright book of life. Books are not life. They are only tremulations on the ether [that is, communications]. But the novel as a tremulation can make the whole man alive tremble. Which is more than poetry, philosophy, science, or any other book tremulations can do.

The essay finishes by arguing against all absolutes and rules, urging that novels teach us how to live, if they are any good. Since he counts not only the Bible, but Shakespeare and Homer – and anything in literature of which he approves – as 'novels', we may assume that Lawrence would want his short stories judged by novelistic criteria: we must ask whether they succeed in going 'the whole hog'.

Specimen questions

Essay questions could be set on many of the above study topics (pp. 59–61). Students should always look closely at the precise wording of a question.

Major topics

---

(1) Discuss symbolism in some of Lawrence's short stories.
(2) How does Lawrence use settings?
(3) Write on the presentation of women in the stories. How well does Lawrence understand women?
(4) Show how characters are contrasted, and explain why.
(5) In what sense can we talk of a story-writer's 'poetic imagination'?
(6) Write on Lawrence's satirical short stories.
(7) Comment on Lawrence's sense of humour.
(8) How effectively do the stories show the place of money in the characters' lives?

(9) Compare two scenes of violence and say what the stories imply about the violence.

(10) 'The whole man and woman alive'. Discuss any two short stories to show what Lawrence means.

Minor topics

(1) Discuss Lawrence's use of costume.
(2) Comment on Lawrence's titles.
(3) Comment on his characters' names.
(4) Write on descriptions, or dialogue, or imagery.
(5) Write on one of the following topics with examples from several stories: children, animals, weather, death, flowers, the seasons, coal-mining, luck.

Specimen answers

Major topics

(1) Discuss symbolism in some of Lawrence's short stories.
Lawrence's symbols reveal his characters. Characters may be conscious or unconscious of symbols, or sometimes instinctively aware of them. The reader must always think of the symbols in relation to the people of the stories.

Elizabeth Bates smells the odour of her chrysanthemums before she puts the flowers in her apron-band, and when the child Annie smells the flowers, in a rapture at their beauty at her mother's waist, the chrysanthemums and their odour seem to speak of life and hope, in contrast to the ugly images of Walter, evoked by Elizabeth's words – dead drunk and lying in his pit-dirt on the floor. But Elizabeth interprets them differently when she tells Annie that her father had chrysanthemums in his button-hole the first time he came home drunk. After the news of her husband's death, the room is filled with 'the cold, deathly smell' of the flowers, and the change seems connected with Elizabeth's brutal words to her child, as though her hatred of her husband had killed the flowers. It seems appropriate, therefore, that when the vase is knocked over she kneels to mop up the water sooner than look at her husband. Flowers signify life and death, in custom, ritual and poetry. In this story the odour of the chrysanthemums connects the mother with her children and her unloved husband, and with the 'cold' infant in her womb. Elizabeth is not aware of all their implications. But she is learning about herself in the last pages, and she may come to remember how she raised to her face in the garden the flowers which were soon to fall beside Walter's body, and the bitterness of her words to Annie, soon to turn to remorse.

Ephraim, in 'Strike-Pay', could not explain to his mother-in-law that he lost his half-sovereign in a symbolic ride on a pit-pony, and she would laugh at any such soft talk. Horses are symbols of vitality and strength in Lawrence, and these ponies, bemused at finding themselves above ground because of the strike, need riding. Ephraim's ride is not the mastering of an animal, but rather the expression of animal high spirits, as he falls off and chases the pony, showing off his stunts. The recklessness of the miners' day out is symbolised in this unsuccessful horse-play. But the story is a comedy, and Lawrence's ideas about instinct and consciousness, body and mind, are only lightly involved. Ephraim's exuberance is more attractive than his mother-in-law's nagging, and his wife forgives him in the end.

'The Man Who Loved Islands' and 'Things' contrast the characters' views on symbols with Lawrence's. The man sees an island as a world to master. The story sees him as an egotist, denying life, studying the flora of antiquity instead of loving Flora, and deserving to suffer self-imprisonment on a rock in the Hebrides. Lawrence thinks the love of islands symbolic of idealism, and means to show that this is a false approach to life, which must end in misanthropy. As Cathcart loses his ideals, his islands diminish, until nothing remains except the elements. The idealists of 'Things' think their Florence house 'entirely furnished by loveliness, not by "things" at all'. 'Chartres!' Valerie exclaims, 'mentally falling on her knees' before the curtains. Lawrence laughs at the Melvilles because he thinks the opposite: their 'things' symbolise the materialism they say they have left America to escape. By the end of the story, Erasmus has taken a job in order to house the 'loveliness', in materialistic Ohio.

Lawrence rightly said that symbols are not invented: they have grown over long eras in human consciousness – flowers, horses, islands and beautiful things are naturally symbolic. But he did discover an unusual and effective symbol in the child's rocking-horse. Woodenly rigid, ugly and mechanical, this indoor plaything is in every respect the opposite of what it represents. It is, therefore, an effective symbol in 'The Rocking-Horse Winner' of all that is unnatural in Paul's crazed ride to riches and death. The boy seems to be unconsciously aware that it symbolises the false, dangerous elements of gambling, when he talks to Uncle Oscar and Bassett of 'going high', in the betting, and 'going down' when he does not 'know', and they lose – as a rocking-horse see-saws up and down.

Symbols can sometimes be a pure, artificial literary device, but in

Lawrence's stories they always serve his purpose of showing what life is like.

Minor topics

(1) Discuss Lawrence's use of costume.

Clothes are a sign language in fiction, as they are, in one of their roles, in life. They often reflect social condition or status. The child John Bates in 'Odour of Chrysanthemums' wears garments of cloth that is 'too thick and hard' for their size – evidently 'cut down' from his father's worn-out clothes. That was once a familiar sight in England. Lawrence conveys a sense of poverty as an unnatural, heavy burden. Fanny is vexed when Harry meets her at the railway station in 'Fanny and Annie' because of his 'common cap' and workman's scarf but no collar. It irritates her that he is unashamed of being a workman and does not try to hide it. Although her family is poor, Louisa is a daughter of the vicar, and in her eyes Alfred looks a workman again as soon as he dresses after his wash. His clothes are poor, and they influence his bearing, imposing on him the air of 'inferiority' which she resents.

Clothes are significant in other ways. Lawrence associates uniforms with male aggression. When the sisters in 'You Touched Me' watch Hadrian swaggering in his soldier's uniform, 'at his ease, as if in possession' of the Pottery House, they sense that he is 'charged with plebeian energy', and they assume at once that he is after their father's money. In 'The Prussian Officer' the Captain's splendid uniform looks even more a sign of aggression. John Thomas's inspector's uniform in 'Tickets, Please', in which he looks 'a fine cock-of-the-walk', is torn to shreds in a scene which can be read as a symbolic killing, parallel to the rending of Pentheus in Euripides. Tearing his tunic, the girls attack his status as a man with authority over them.

The stories show women's sensitivity to clothes. Matilda in 'You Touched Me' is mortified when Hadrian arrives too soon, catching her with her hair 'coquettishly' tied up in a duster. Later she dresses to assert herself, with a 'long string of exquisite crystal beads over her soft green dress'. Lawrence comments tartly on her elegance: 'now she looked elegant, like a heroine in a magazine illustration, and almost as unreal'. Much more real, in Lawrence's world, are the uniforms of the tram-conductresses:

> The girls are fearless young hussies. In their ugly blue uniform, skirts up to their knees, shapeless old peaked caps on their heads, they have all the *sang-froid* of an old non-commissioned officer.

Such girls, who took over jobs from men who had gone to fight, were a new phenomenon in the last years of the First World War. Lawrence seems to approve, as we would expect, of their emancipation: their short skirts and men's caps and manners, and their claiming the dignity of an adventurous kind of work. The story also shows women's vulnerability, treating the bravado of the 'hussies' in a comic spirit, and the 'mute, stupefied faces' at the end more gravely.

Lawrence's characters frequently appear naked, partly or wholly. Stripped for washing, Alfred looks wonderful to Louisa. Lawrence always wanted to remind us that clothes are no part of 'the man or woman alive'.

(2) Comment on Lawrence's titles.
Some titles seem inevitable. 'Things' could be called nothing else. 'Odour of Chrysanthemums' emphasises the central symbol, and is a reminder that it is the 'odour', more than the flowers themselves, 'deathly and mysterious', which we must have in mind. 'You Touched Me' is an improvement on Lawrence's first idea for a title, 'Hadrian', although that character's name is well chosen. 'Hadrian' sounds rather institutional, since it is not a name many parents would choose: we may reflect that the emperor after whom the wall, built in the second century AD to keep the Picts out of Roman Britain, is named, came as an invader, as Lawrence's character comes. We may reflect too that he is a character who wants to keep on his own side of a social wall. But the 'touch' is crucial in this story, as the final title says.

Lawrence's first title for 'Tickets, Please' was 'John Thomas'. Like the nickname 'Monkey Nuts', this looks innocent but also has a sexual meaning. Resentful of the censorship which prevented his use of taboo words in his published fiction, Lawrence enjoyed phrases of this kind. The editor of the *Strand* magazine, where it first appeared, rejected even 'John Thomas'. 'Tickets, Please' is a better title anyway, appropriate for trams and full of other connotations, of the theatre, of a lottery, and so on. 'The Man Who Loved Islands' has the proper ring for a fable. Some titles sound respectable and religious – 'The Christening', 'Daughters of the Vicar' – although their stories actually attack middle-class, Christian respectability. They also sound old-fashioned. Some critics have pointed out that although Lawrence's work was original in many ways, it was conventional in others. Occasions such as a christening were the basis for nineteenth-century short stories, and two sisters looking out from a vicarage for husbands is a classic situation in English fiction.

Part 5
Suggestions for further reading

THE STORIES treated in Parts 2 and 3 of these Notes are those collected in *D. H. Lawrence: Selected Tales*, introduced by Ian Serraillier, New Windmill Series, Heinemann Educational Books, London, 1963. *D. H. Lawrence: Selected Short Stories*, edited with introduction and notes by Brian Finney, Penguin Twentieth Century Classics, Penguin Books, Harmondsworth, 1982, is a more ample collection, which contains the stories discussed only in Part 4, as well as a number of others.

Other works by D. H. Lawrence

Lawrence wrote over fifty books. Most are available in hardback, published by Heinemann, London, and in paperback, published by Penguin Books, Harmondsworth. The following titles are recommended for beginners: *The White Peacock*, 1911; *Sons and Lovers*, 1913; *The Prussian Officer*, 1914 (short stories); *The Rainbow*, 1915; *Twilight in Italy*, 1916 (travel); *England, My England*, 1922 (short stories); *The Ladybird, The Fox, The Captain's Doll*, 1923; *St Mawr*, 1925; *The Woman Who Rode Away*, 1928 (short stories); *Lady Chatterley's Lover*, Florence, 1928; London, 1960; *The Virgin and the Gipsy*, 1930; *The Lovely Lady*, 1933 (short stories); *Phoenix: the Posthumous Papers*, edited by Edward D. McDonald, 1936; *Selected Letters*, edited by Richard Aldington, 1950; *Phoenix II: Uncollected, Unpublished and Other Prose Works*, edited by Warren Roberts and Harry T. Moore, 1968; *The Complete Poems*, edited by Vivian de Sola Pinto and Warren Roberts, 1964.

Biography and criticism

ALCORN, JOHN: *The Nature Novel from Hardy to Lawrence*, Macmillan, London, 1977.

ALLDRITT, KEITH: *The Visual Imagination of D. H. Lawrence*, Edward Arnold, London, 1971.

BEAL, ANTHONY: *D. H. Lawrence* (Writers and Critics Series), Oliver & Boyd, Edinburgh, 1961.

COOMBES, H. (ED.): *D. H. Lawrence: A Critical Anthology*, Penguin Books, Harmondsworth, 1973.

HOUGH, GRAHAM: *The Dark Sun*, Duckworth, London, 1973.

KERMODE, FRANK: *Lawrence*, Fontana Collins, London, 1973.

LEAVIS, F. R.: *D. H. Lawrence: Novelist*, Chatto & Windus, London, 1955; Penguin Books, Harmondsworth, 1973.

MOORE, HARRY T.: *The Priest of Love: A Life of D. H. Lawrence*, revised edition, Heinemann, London, 1974; Penguin Books, Harmondsworth, 1976.

NEHLS, EDWARD H.: *D. H. Lawrence: A Composite Biography*, 3 vols, University of Wisconsin Press, Madison, 1957–9.

PRITCHARD, R. E.: *D. H. Lawrence: Body of Darkness*, Hutchinson, London, 1971.

SAGAR, KEITH: *The Art of D. H. Lawrence*, Cambridge University Press, Cambridge, 1966.

SAGAR, KEITH: *D. H. Lawrence: An Illustrated Biography*, Eyre Methuen, London, 1980.

STEWART, J. I. M.: *Eight Modern Writers*, Clarendon Press, Oxford, 1963.

TIVERTON, FATHER WILLIAM (FATHER MARTIN JARRETT-KERR): *D. H. Lawrence and Human Experience*, Rockliff, London, 1951.

WILLIAMS, RAYMOND: *The English Novel from Dickens to Lawrence*, Chatto & Windus, London, 1970; Paladin, St Albans, 1974.

YOUNG, KENNETH: *D. H. Lawrence* (Writers and their Work), Longman for the British Council, Harlow, 1952, 1969.

The author of these notes

NEIL MCEWAN read English at Pembroke College, Oxford. He has taught English Literature at universities in Canada, England, Cameroon, Morocco and Qatar, and is now Lecturer in English at Okayama University, Japan. He is the author of *The Survival of the Novel*, (Macmillan, London, 1981); *Africa and the Novel* (Macmillan, 1983); *Perspective in British Historical Fiction Today* (Macmillan, 1987); *Graham Greene*, 'Macmillan Modern Novelists' (Macmillan, 1988); and is the editor of Volume 5, *The Twentieth Century*, of the *Macmillan Anthologies of English Literature* (1989). His *Anthony Powell*, in the 'Macmillan Modern Novelists' series, is soon to be published. In York Handbooks, he has written *Preparing for Examinations in English Literature* (1984) and *Style in English Prose* (1986). His many titles in York Notes include *D. H. Lawrence: Women in Love* (1981), *Ted Hughes: Selected Poems* (1990), and *Keith Waterhouse: Billy Liar* (1990).